CONTENTS

how2become

how2become

A Train Conductor
The Insider's Guide

Richard McMunn

Orders: Please contact How2become Ltd, Suite 2, 50 Churchill Square Business Centre, Kings Hill, Kent ME19 4YU. You can also order via the e mail address info@how2become.co.uk.

ISBN: 9781909229679

First published 2013

Typeset for How2become Ltd by Molly Hill, Canada.

Printed in Great Britain for How2become Ltd by Bell & Bain Ltd, 303 Burnfield Road, Thornliebank, Glasgow G46 7UQ.

INTRODUCTION

Dear Sir/Madam,

Welcome to how2become a Train Conductor: The Insider's Guide. This guide has been designed to help you prepare for and pass the Train Conductor selection process. We feel certain that you will find the guide both a comprehensive and highly informative tool for helping you to obtain this much sought after career.

The Train Conductor selection process is not easy to pass. Many people apply to become train conductors as they want to gain experience working for a Train Operating Company before progressing to the role of a train driver. You must prepare fully if you are to pass the selection process and be offered a position as a train conductor. There are a number of things that you can do in order to increase your chances of success, and they are all contained within this guide. The majority of Train Operating Companies (TOCs) are both professional and meticulous in how they run their assessment centres and you should find the process an enjoyable one. We hope that you enjoy the guide and we wish you all the best in your pursuit of becoming a conductor.

If you would like any further assistance with the selection process then we offer many other products and training courses via our website www.how2become.com. Finally, you won't achieve much in life without hard work, determination and perseverance. Work hard, stay focused and be what you want!

Good luck and best wishes,

The how2become team

The How2become team

how2become

PREFACE BY AUTHOR RICHARD McMUNN

Before I get into the guide and teach you how to prepare for the train conductor selection process, it is important that I explain a little bit about my background and why I am qualified to help you succeed.

I joined the Royal Navy soon after leaving school and spent four fabulous years in the Fleet Air Arm branch on-board HMS Invincible. It had always been my dream to become a Firefighter and I only ever intended to stay in the Royal Navy for the minimum amount of time. At the age of 21 I left the Royal Navy and joined Kent Fire and Rescue Service. Over the next 17 years I had an amazing career with a fantastic organisation. During that time I was heavily involved in training and recruitment, often sitting on interview panels and marking application forms for those people who wanted to become Firefighters. I also worked very hard and rose to the rank of Station Manager. I passed numerous assessment centres during my time in the job and I estimate that I was successful at over 95% of interviews I attended.

 how2become

The reason for my success was not because I am special in anyway, or that I have lots of educational qualifications, because I don't! In the build-up to every job application or promotion I always prepared myself thoroughly. I found a formula that worked and that is what I intend to teach you throughout the duration of this book.

Over the past few years I have taught many people how to pass the selection process for becoming both Train Conductors and also Trainee Train Drivers. As you are probably aware many people want to become Train Conductors. As a result of this, the competition can be quite fierce. However, the vast majority of people who do apply will submit poor application forms or they will do very little to prepare for the assessment centre and the interview. As a result, they will fail.

The way to pass the selection process is to embark on a comprehensive period of intense preparation. I would urge you to use an action plan during your preparation. This will allow you to focus your mind on exactly what you need to do in order to pass. For example, if it has been many years since you last attended an interview, then you will probably have a lot of work to do in this area. If it has been many years since you last sat a test, then you may have to work very hard in order to pass the psychometric tests that form part of the assessment centre. The point I am making here, is that it is within your power to improve on your weak areas. If you use an action plan then you are far more likely to achieve your goals.

I use action plans in just about every element of my work. Action plans work simply because they focus your mind on what needs to be done. Once you have created your action plan, stick it in a prominent position such as your fridge door. This will act as a reminder of the work that you need to do in order to prepare properly for selection. Your action plan might look something like this:

Monday	Tuesday	Wednesday	Thursday	Friday
Research into the TOC I am applying for. Includes reading recruitment literature and visiting websites.	60 minute Interview preparation including preparing my responses to questions.	Obtain application form and read recruitment literature and application form guidance notes.	Research into the TOC I am applying for. Includes reading recruitment literature and visiting websites.	60 minute mock interview with a friend or relative.
60 minutes preparation on document sales tests and also the document audit test.	30 minute Dots Concentration Test preparation.	45 minute reading up on the role of a train conductor and the job description/person specification.	60 minutes preparation on document sales tests and also the document audit test.	30 minute Dots Concentration Test preparation.
20 minute jog or brisk walk.	30 minutes gym work.	REST PERIOD – no fitness or exercise.	20 minute jog or brisk walk.	30 minutes gym work.

Note: Saturday and Sunday, rest days.

The above sample action plan is just a simple example of what you may wish to include. Your action plan will very much depend on your strengths and weaknesses. After reading this guide, decide which areas you need to work on and then add them to your action plan. Areas that you may wish to include in your action plan could be:

- Researching the role of a Train Conductor;

- Researching the training that you will undergo as a Train Conductor and the necessary requirements of the role;

- Researching the Train Operating Company that you are applying for;

- Dedicating time to completing the application form and reading the guidance notes;

- Carrying out practice tests that are similar to the ones required at the assessment centre in regards to the ticket selling exam and also the ticket checking exam;

- Light fitness work in order to keep up your concentration levels and improve your positive state of mind;

- Interview preparation including carrying out a mock interview.

You will note that throughout the duration of this guide I make continued reference to 'preparation'. During my career I have been successful at over 95% of interviews and assessments that I've attended. The reason for this is simply because I always embark on a period of focused preparation, and I always aim to improve on my weak areas. Follow this simple process and you too can enjoy the same levels of success that I have enjoyed.

Finally, it is very important that you believe in your own abilities. It does not matter if you have no qualifications. It does not matter if you have no knowledge yet of the role of a Train Conductor. What does matter is self-belief, self-discipline and a genuine desire to improve and become successful.

Enjoy reading the guide and then set out on a period of intense preparation!

Best wishes,

Richard McMunn

Richard McMunn

DISCLAIMER

Every effort has been made to ensure that the information contained within this guide is accurate at the time of publication. How2become Ltd is not responsible for anyone failing any part of any selection process as a result of the information contained within this guide. How2become Ltd and their authors cannot accept any responsibility for any errors or omissions within this guide, however caused. No responsibility for loss or damage occasioned by any person acting, or refraining from action, as a result of the material in this publication can be accepted by How2become Ltd.

The information within this guide does not represent the views of any third party service or organisation.

CHAPTER ONE
THE ROLE OF A TRAIN CONDUCTOR

Conductors operate at the very heart of the service provided by Train Operating Companies. Train Conductors are the first person the passenger will see and, more often than not, the first person from the TOC that the passenger will speak to. Therefore, it is absolutely vital that the Conductor is capable of providing an excellent level of customer service. Whilst there are many different facets to the role of a Conductor customer service is right at the top of the list alongside safety.

To make sure the trains run both safely and on time, a train operating company will need people who can handle a wide range of responsibilities while remaining customer-focused and approachable.

As a Conductor you will need to be highly customer orientated, answering queries, assisting with boarding, seating and

 how2become

overcrowding on the trains, providing accurate information and above all, promoting a feeling of safety, security and a first class service to all of the passengers travelling on the train.

In addition, you will undertake other important duties such as examining and issuing tickets, communicating with passengers over the train announcement system and checking the train is safe and comfortable inside.

Many Train Operating Companies operate a 24-hour service, therefore, having the ability to be flexible is absolutely crucial to the role. This means that your shift lengths and patterns will most certainly vary and will include early starts, late finishes, weekend and bank holiday working. To comply with UK Working Time legislation, you'll need to be at least 18 years of age, medically fit, and have perfect colour vision in order to apply. Whilst no formal qualifications are needed, Train Operators are looking for people who can demonstrate an interest in customer services, who enjoy working with the general public and who have experience of shift-work. You must be able to work unsupervised, be conscientious and honest and be able to deal with unexpected situations as and when they arise.

THE RECRUITMENT PROCESS

APPLICATION FORM

This is the first stage of the selection process and one of the toughest stages to get through, simply because there will be so many people applying for the post. Having said that, I can confidently state that the vast majority of people applying will be poorly prepared and their form will not be accepted. Whilst I will go in to greater details later on about

the application form, it will generally consist of the following areas:

- General personal details
- Employment history
- Education and qualifications
- References
- Personal development
- Customer service experience
- Handling difficult situations experience
- Communication skills
- Motivation
- Equal opportunities
- CV upload
- Drugs and alcohol statement
- Declaration

Many of the sections on the application form are relatively easy to pass; however, some of the sections such as customer service experience, handling difficult situations experience and communication skills require you to provide EVIDENCE of where you have previously demonstrated that particular quality. Later on within this guide I will teach you exactly how to answer these questions correctly.

Most Train Operating Companies will require you to apply and submit your application for the role online, so it is important that you have access to a computer and internet access.

INTERVIEW

Once short listed, you may be invited to attend a selection interview, either by telephone or face-to-face. This is so that the TOC can get to know you better and learn more about your suitability for the job. They will also ask you questions about how you would deal with certain scenarios if you were a Conductor. They will then decide on the basis of the interview, whether to progress you to the next stage of the recruitment process, which is usually an assessment centre. Please note, some TOC's will require you to attend the assessment centre prior to the interview, so please do check first before using this information.

ASSESSMENT CENTRE

If you are invited to attend the assessment centre, it will usually take place around one week after the selection interview. The assessment centre is designed specifically to help the Train Operating Company to select the best people for the job. You will be asked to sit a number of paper-and-pencil exercises and undertake a structured interview. During this day, they will further assess your ability to succeed in the job. In particular they will be looking at your ability to deal with ticket checks/sales, your concentration skills and your ability to deal with unexpected situations.

The Train Operating Company will normally send you practice materials in advance to help prepare you for the day.

HOW AND WHERE TO APPLY

Most TOCs will advertise their vacancies either on their website or in the local press/media. Some TOCs provide an

e-mail notification service that will inform you of any vacancies that become available, so it is certainly worth visiting their website to see if this type of service exists. Within the 'Useful Contacts' section of this guide I have provided you with the contact details for many of the Train Operating Companies.

In a nutshell, TOCs advertise vacancies as and when they become available. Train Conductor vacancies are advertised more frequently than Trainee Train Driver posts, simply because there are usually more opportunities within this type of role. In terms of applying for vacancies, many TOCs now only allow you to apply on-line. You may also have to upload your CV when submitting your application form, so don't forget to check out the section within this guide that relates to creating CV's before doing so as the CV will carry a lot of weight during the scoring of your application form.

CHAPTER TWO

MY TOP INSIDER TIPS AND ADVICE FOR SUCCESS

TIP 1 – BE PATIENT, PERSISTENT AND ALWAYS LOOK FOR WAYS TO IMPROVE ON YOUR WEAK AREAS

Many popular jobs, including the job of a Train Conductor, are difficult to obtain. There are a number of reasons for this but the main one is the competition. Many people will apply for the position of Conductor, so you need to stand out from the crowd in order to progress through each stage. Ask yourself how serious you are about becoming a Train Conductor? Are you prepared to keep trying if you fail at one of the stages? Are you prepared to work hard to improve yourself and take the time required to prepare for the selection process?

The main thing to remember is that you can achieve your goal of becoming a Train Conductor, providing you are prepared

to work hard and improve. There are many ways of improving your chances of success and this guide will help you to understand them. I would strongly advise that you utilise an action plan to help you concentrate on your weaker areas. Whilst I have already covered this during the early stage of the guide, it is worth mentioning it again. Within your action plan try to include lots of focus on your weak areas. Let's say for example you are not confident at your ability to pass the ticket selling exam which forms part of the assessment day. Within your action plan you will need to write down exactly what you plan to do in order to improve in this weak area – then take action. This may include:

- Carrying out 20 minutes worth of timed tests five nights per week that will help to improve your scores at the assessment centre.

- Obtaining further practice booklets with sample test questions. I recommend my Dots Concentration testing book which is available through Amazon.co.uk or How2become.com.

- Employing the services of a personal tutor, if required.

The key to improvement is to carry out what I call 'deliberate and repetitive' practice. This effectively means finding out exactly what you are weak at, and then carrying out lots of targeted practice until you can do it with your eyes closed! Not literally, but hopefully you get my point.

TIP 2 – LEARN ABOUT THE TRAIN OPERATING COMPANY YOU ARE APPLYING FOR

Put yourself in the shoes of the recruitment officer of the Train Operating Company you are applying to join. What type of person do you want to employ as a Train Conductor?

Someone who is serious about joining your TOC? Or someone who is just applying to any TOC with the sole purpose of securing a position as a Train Conductor? The answer should be obvious. Therefore, you need to learn about the TOC you are applying to join in order to increase your chances of success.

During my research into this guide I spoke to a number of recruitment officers from different Train Operating Companies and they all said the same thing – "You can spot a serial applicant a mile off!" A serial applicant is someone who applies for every job regardless of the TOC. Whilst there is nothing wrong with this, there is a danger of that particular applicant not spending sufficient time on his or her application form and subsequently submitting a weak application.

When you complete the application form you will have the opportunity to make reference to the reasons why you want to become a Train Conductor with that particular company. Throughout this guide I will show you how to increase your chances of success and demonstrate whether or not you are serious about joining a TOC.

TIP 3 – PRACTICE PLENTY OF TEST QUESTIONS

You'd be surprised at how many candidates attend the assessment centre having carried out little or no preparation whatsoever. Don't be one of those people who are ill-prepared.

The selection process involves a number of different tests. The more common ones that are in use include:

- A ticket selling exam;

- A ticket checking exam;

- A concentration test;
- Role play assessments.

There are a number of ways that you can increase your chances of success and within this guide I will show you how. Some of people who fail the assessment do so during the concentration tests. The majority of tests require you to concentrate on a repetitive and monotonous task for a prolonged period of time. Although the test itself appears to be relatively simple, it is in fact difficult to master. Train Operating Companies need to be 100% sure that you can concentrate for long periods of time whilst carrying out repetitive tasks.

In addition to practicing the sample tests that I have provided within this guide, I strongly encourage you to obtain additional testing books and resources. Just by practicing different psychometric tests your brain will begin to work quicker and more effectively and it is important that you take the time to do this. Make sure you allocate plenty of time in your action plan to each of the testing areas indicated above.

TIP 4 – UNDERSTAND THE IMPORTANCE OF BEING 'CUSTOMER FOCUSED'

All Train Operating Companies are competing to provide a high level of customer service. In any business it is the quality and reliability of service that will bring the customer back time and time again. Try to think of a shop or company that you have had a good experience with. What was so special about them that would make you go back to them? Most probably the level of customer service is the reason why.

When you apply to become a Train Conductor you need to demonstrate a good 'customer-focused' attitude. You can demonstrate this both on your application form and during

the interview. TOCs want the people who work for them to provide the highest level of customer service possible so that the customer comes back to them time and time again. An unhappy customer is likely to tell ten other people about their bad experience, so the knock on effect can be huge. Think about the importance of being customer-focused and make it a prominent part of your application. If you have any previous experience of working in a customer-focused role then I advise that you include this on your application form.

TIP 5 – DEMONSTRATE AN AWARENESS OF SAFETY

Being safe and having the ability to follow safety rules and regulations is crucial to the role. Safety must always come first! As a fully qualified Train Conductor you have a lot of responsibility in relation to safety rules and procedures. If you cannot follow these rules and procedures, then you will not make a competent Conductor.

Throughout the selection process you will be assessed against this important area and it is essential that you have it at the forefront of your mind at all times. When completing the application form you may be asked to provide an example of where you have been responsible for safety, or where safety has played an important part in a group or individual task. Think about your responses carefully and include answers that demonstrate your knowledge and understanding of the importance of safety. If you have any experience of carrying out a safety conscious role during current or previous employment then I would advise that you include this in your application form responses.

To learn more about safety in the workplace take a look at the Government's own Health and Safety website. This can be found at the following web address – www.hse.gov.uk

 how2become

TIP 6 – BE SMART AND PRESENTABLE

It goes without saying, but you'd be amazed at how many people turn up to the assessment centre, and even the interview, in jeans and a t-shirt! Unsurprisingly, this does not go down well with the recruitment staff.

You are applying for a highly sought after post with a Train Operating Company that most probably sets itself high standards. Therefore, it is important that you set yourself high standards right from the offset. Whenever you come into contact with the TOC or recruitment staff, you should always ensure that you are wearing formal clothing in the form of shirt and tie for men or smart dress for women. Make sure you are clean shaven and that your shoes are clean and tidy. You only get one chance to make a first impression so make sure it's a positive one.

Another piece of important advice is not to be late for any of your appointments. It is far better to arrive 15 minutes early than 1 minute late. There is a big emphasis by TOCs on ensuring their trains run on time. Therefore, they want to employ Train Conductors who are capable of getting to work on time.

TIP 7 – TOC FIRST, TRAIN CONDUCTOR SECOND

As you can imagine, many applicants are not too bothered which Train Operating Company they work for, so long as they get to become a Train Conductor! In my view this is a mistake and it will not assist them in their application. Throughout the application process you should demonstrate that you have a desire to join that particular TOC, as opposed to being hell bent on simply becoming a Train Conductor. The way to achieve this is to learn just as much about the TOC you are

applying for as you do about the role of a Train Conductor. During the interview there is a strong possibility that you will be asked questions similar to the following:

Q. Why do you want to work for our company?

Q. What research have you carried out into our company?

Q. What significant events have happened in this TOC over the past 12 months?

Q. What has attracted you to our company?

During your preparation for becoming a Train Conductor make sure you carry out plenty of research into the TOC.

CHAPTER THREE

HOW TO CREATE AN
EFFECTIVE CV

As I discussed earlier in the guide, you may be required to upload your CV when you apply to become a Train Conductor. During this section of the guide I will provide you with a step-by-step guide on how to create a CV that is both effective and relevant to the TOC you want to join.

The word Curriculum Vitae translated means the 'course of life'. CV's are used to demonstrate to an employer that you have the potential, the skills, and the experience to carry out the role you are applying for. Your CV is a very important document and you should spend sufficient time designing it so that it matches the job that you are applying for as closely as possible.

WHAT MAKES AN EFFECTIVE CV?

In simple terms an effective CV is one that matches the specification and the requirements of the job you are applying for. Your CV should be used as a tool to assist you in your application for becoming a Train Conductor and it should be centred on the following areas:

- Creating the right impression of yourself;

- Indicating that you possess the right qualities and attributes to perform the role;

- Grabbing the Train Operating Company's attention;

- Being concise and clear.

The most effective CV's are the ones that make the assessor's job easy. They are simple to read, to the point, relevant and focus on the job/role that you are applying for. CV's should not be overly long unless an employer specifically asks for this. Effective CV writing is an acquired skill that can be obtained relatively quickly with a little bit of time, effort and focus.

Before you begin to start work on your CV it is a good idea to have a basic idea of how a job/person specification is constructed. A job description/person specification is basically a blueprint for the role you are applying for; it sets out what the employer expects from potential applicants. One of your main focus points during the construction of your CV will be to match the job/person specification of the Train Conductor. Most job/person specifications will include the following areas:

EXPERIENCE REQUIRED: previous jobs, unpaid work experience, life experience, skills, knowledge and abilities:

for example, languages, driving, knowledge of specialist fields, ability to use equipment, plus some indication of the level of competence required, and whether the person must have the skills or knowledge beforehand or can learn them on the job.

QUALIFICATIONS REQUIRED: exams, certificates, degrees, diplomas (some jobs require specific qualifications, but most do not and it can be fairer to ask for the skills or knowledge represented by the qualification rather than asking for the qualification itself).

PERSONAL ATTRIBUTES REQUIRED: such as ability to concentrate, a willingness to work on one's own and the ability to work within a team environment.

PERSONAL CIRCUMSTANCES: such as residing in a certain area and being able to work weekends or evenings.

Most job/person specifications will be based around a task analysis of the vacancy, so there should be nothing within the job description/person specification that is irrelevant or that does not concern the particular role you are applying for. Whatever requirements you are asked to meet, you should try hard to match them as closely as possible, providing evidence if possible of your previous experience.

WHAT IS THE TOC LOOKING FOR IN YOUR CV?

As previously stated you should ensure that you make the assessor's job as simple as possible. Try to put yourself in the shoes of the assessor. How would you want an applicant's CV to look? You would want it to be relevant to role they are applying for and you would want it to be neat, concise and well organised. You need to spend some time thinking

about the type of person the TOC are looking for and how you can match the specification that is relevant to the job you want. Most job specifications will list the essential/ desirable requirements in terms of education, qualifications, training, experience, skills, personality and any other special requirements.

Let's take a look at some of the skills required to become a Train Conductor. Please note, the following details are not relevant to any particular TOC and you may find that requirements vary for each different company.

DUTIES, SKILLS AND KNOWLEDGE REQUIRED TO BECOME A TRAIN CONDUCTOR

As a Conductor, your day-to-day duties would include:

- Checking the carriages are clean before the start of a journey;
- Making sure equipment, doors and controls are working properly;
- Walking through carriages during the journey, checking tickets and travel documents;
- Answering passengers' questions about routes, arrival times and connections;
- Making announcements over the public address system;
- Making sure passengers get on and off the train safely;
- Dealing with unexpected delays or emergencies, for example a passenger falling ill;
- You would also write reports, detailing any delays or incidents that occur during each journey.

Skills and knowledge:

- Excellent customer service skills;

- A pleasant manner and smart appearance;

- A good understanding of rail regulations, safety procedures, fares and timetables;

- A clear speaking voice for making passenger announcements;

- The ability to accept responsibility and work without supervision;

- The ability to deal professionally with upset or angry passengers;

- Good math's skills for handling cash and payments;

- A willingness to work flexibly.

You will see from the above details that some of the key elements of the role include an ability to carry out checks, follow rules and procedures, a level of self-discipline, be capable of dealing with people and knowledge of rail regulations. Once you have the above information then you will be able to mould your CV around the key aspects of the job.

Before I provide you with a sample CV that is based on matching the above role, let's first of all take a look at some of the key elements of a CV.

THE KEY ELEMENTS OF A CV

The following is a list of information I recommend you include within your CV. Try to put them in this order and remember to be brief and to the point. Make sure you include and highlight

the positive aspects of your experience and achievements.

- Your personal details
- Your profile
- Your employment history
- Your academic acievements
- Your interests
- Any other information
- Your references

Let's now take a look at each of the above sections and what you need to include.

YOUR PERSONAL DETAILS

When completing this section you should include the following details:

- Your full name
- Address
- Date of birth
- Nationality
- Contact telephone numbers including home and mobile
- E mail address

PROFILE

To begin with try to write a brief but to the point statement about yourself making sure you include the keywords that best describe your character. Some effective words to use

when describing you might include:

Ambitious, enthusiastic, safety conscious, customer-focused, motivated, flexible, caring, trustworthy, meticulous, sense of humour, drive, character, determination, will to succeed, passionate, loyal, teamwork, hard working.

The above words are all powerful and positive aspects of an individual's character. Try to think of your own character and what positive words you can use that best describe you.

Within your profile description try to include a statement that is relative to you and that will make the TOC think you are the right person for the job, such as:

"I am an extremely conscientious and hard working person who has a great deal of experience in customer service. I have very good organisational and motivational skills and I am always striving to improve myself. I believe that I would embrace the challenges that this new role has to offer and I am able to learn large amounts of job relevant information and procedures."

EMPLOYMENT HISTORY

When completing this section try to ensure that it is completed in reverse chronological order. Provide the reader with dates, locations and employers, and remember to include your job title. Give a brief description of your main achievements and try to include words of a positive nature, such as:

Achieved, developed, progressed, managed, created, succeeded, devised, drove, expanded, directed.

It is also a good idea to quantify your main achievements, such as:

"During my time with this employer I was responsible for carrying out difficult tasks whilst under pressure."

ACADEMIC ACHIEVEMENTS

When completing this section include the dates, names and locations of the schools, colleges or universities that you attended in chronological order.

You should also include your qualifications and any other relevant achievements such as health and safety qualifications, customer service courses and/or first aid qualifications. Anything that is relevant to the role you're applying for would be an advantage.

INTERESTS

Within this section try to include interests that match the requirements of the job and ones that also portray you in a positive manner. Maybe you have worked within the voluntary sector or have even carried out some charity work in the past? If so, try to include these in your CV as they show you have a caring and concerning nature. In relation to the role of a Train Conductor, the following activities and past times are recommended:

- Playing a team sport or activity. This demonstrates you have the ability to work with others as part of a team.

- Recent study activities such as learning a new qualification. This demonstrates that you are able to learn and retain a large amount of job specific information.

- Playing a musical instrument. This demonstrates you

have the ability to learn something new and that you also have the patience and determination to succeed and an ability to concentrate.

OTHER INFORMATION

Within this section of your CV you can include any other information that is relevant to your skills or experiences that you may feel are of benefit. Examples of these could be certificates of achievement from school or work.

REFERENCES

Within this section try to include your current or previous employer, providing you know that they are going to write positive things about you. Be careful who you choose as a reference and make sure you seek their permission first prior to putting down their name and contact details. It may also be a good idea to ask them if you can have a copy of what they have written about you for reference later.

SAMPLE CV

The following sample CV has been designed to give you an idea of how an effective CV might look. It has been created with the position of Train Conductor in mind. All of the information provided is fictitious.

Curriculum Vitae of
Richard McMunn

Address: 75, Any Street, Anytown, Anyshire. ANY 123
Date of birth: 01/01/1970
Nationality: British
Telephone contact: 01227 XXXXX / Mobile 07890 XXX XXX
E Mail contact: richardmcmunn@anyemailaddress.co.uk

Personal profile of
Richard McMunn

I am an extremely fit and active person who has a great passion for the Rail industry and I have a track record of high achievement. I have very good organisational, motivational and customer service skills and I am always striving to improve myself. I believe that I would embrace the challenges that this new role has to offer. I am a motivated, dedicated, loyal, flexible, conscientious and ambitious person who has the ability to work both within a team and also unsupervised.

I already have a large amount of experience in the working environment and take on a large number of responsibilities both at work, around the home and in my leisure time activities. I currently hold a Health and Safety qualification and I am fully aware of the importance of safety in the role that I am applying for. I have experience in a customer service environment and have the ability to act as a role model for the Train Operating Company. I understand that the role of a Tran Conductor does not just involve selling and checking tickets but it also means acting as a point of contact for the passengers and providing them with an excellent service at all times.

To conclude, I am a fit, motivated, active, organised and professional individual who has a lot of skills and experiences to offer this Train Operating Company.

Employment history of
Richard McMunn
(in chronological order)

Job position/title/company #1   **Date of employment**
goes here   **goes here**
During my time with this employer I was responsible for motivating my team and organising different activities.

Job position/title/company #2   **Date of employment**
goes here   **goes here**
During my time with this employer I was responsible for stock taking and dealing with customer's queries and complaints. I also took on the responsibility of arranging the company's annual staff leisure activity event which often included some form of motivational talk.

Job position/title/company #3   **Date of employment**
goes here   **goes here**
During my time with this employer I undertook a training course in health and safety and first aid. Part of my role included managing resources and carrying out risk assessments as and when required.

Academic achievements of
Richard McMunn

Health and Safety   Date of achievement goes here

First Aid qualification   Date of achievement goes here

GSCE Maths Grade C   Date of achievement goes here

GCSE English Grade C   Date of achievement goes here

GCSE Physical Education   Date of achievement goes here
Grade B

Interests and Hobbies of
Richard McMunn

I am an extremely fit and active person who carries out a structured training programme at my local gym five times a week. During my training sessions I will carry out a variety of different exercises such as indoor rowing, cycling, treadmill work and light weights. I measure my fitness levels by performing the multi-stage fitness test once a week and I can currently achieve level 14.5. In addition to my gym work I am a keen swimmer and break up my gym sessions with long swim sessions twice a week. I can swim 60 lengths of my local swimming pool in time of 35 minutes.

I am also the Captain of my local football team and play in the position of midfield. I am also responsible for organising and arranging the weekly training sessions.

In addition to my sporting activities I like to relax with a weekly Yoga group at my local community centre. I also have a keen interest in art and attend evening classes during the months October through to December.

Further information

Six months ago I decided to carry out a sponsored fitness event in order to raise money for a local charity. I swam 60 lengths of my local swimming pool, and then ran 26 miles before cycling 110 miles all in one day. In total I managed to raise over £10,000 for charity.

References

Name, address and contact details of reference #1

Name, address and contact details of reference #2

TOP TIPS FOR CREATING AN EFFECTIVE CV

New application = new CV
It is important that every time you apply for a job you re-evaluate the content of your CV so that you can match the skills and qualifications required. As a rule you should complete a new CV for every job application unless your applications are close together and the job/person specification is relatively the same. Don't become complacent or allow your CV to get out of date.

Don't pad out your CV
There is a common misconception amongst many job applicants that you need to make your CV scores of pages long for it to get recognised. This simply isn't true. When creating your CV aim for quality rather than quantity. If I was looking through an applicant's CV then I would much prefer to see three to five pages of high quality focused information rather than thirty pages padded out with irrelevance.

Create a positive image
Writing an effective CV involves a number of important aspects. One of those is the manner in which you present your CV. When developing your CV ask yourself the following questions:

- Is the spelling, grammar and punctuation correct?

- Is it legible and easy to read?

- Is the style in which you are writing your CV standardised?

- Is it neat?

- Is it constructed in a logical manner?

By following the above tips in respect of your CV image you will be on the right track, excuse the pun, to improving your chances of getting a job as a Train Conductor. You should spend just as much time on the presentation of your CV as you do on the content.

Do you have the right qualities and attributes for the job you are applying for?

When you are developing your CV have a look at the required personal qualities that are listed within the job/person spec. Try to match these as closely as possible but again, ensure that you provide examples where appropriate. For example, the job description for a Train Conductor includes the following requirements of the role:

"Train conductors are required to check the tickets of our rail passengers to make sure they have paid their fare."

Try and provide an example of where you have achieved this in any previous roles. The following is a fictitious example of how this might be achieved:

> *"In my current role as a delivery driver I am responsible for checking that all goods I pick up from the depot are present and correct. This requires an ability to check that the goods are present, correct and that they have the relevant delivery date and bar code attached to them. It is very important that I deliver the rights goods to the right destination."*

Matching your qualities and attributes to the role you are applying for is very important.

Be honest when creating your CV

If you lie on your CV, especially when it comes to academic qualifications or experience, you will almost certainly get

caught out at some point in the future. Maybe not straight away but even a few months or years down the line an employer can still dismiss you for incorrect information that you provide during the selection process. It simply isn't worth it. Be honest when creating your CV and if you don't have the right skills for the job you are applying for, then go out there and get them!

Now that I've shown you how to create an effective CV, schedule into your action plan a date and time when you intend to create your own. Now let's move on to how to complete the application form correctly.

CHAPTER FOUR
HOW TO COMPLETE THE APPLICATION FORM

THE APPLICATION FORM

Train Operating Company application forms vary. However, the types of questions that you will be asked to respond to are relatively similar in nature. In this section of the guide I have provided you with hints, tips and advice on how to increase your chances of progressing through this important stage. Follow the guidance that I have provided you within this section and your chances will greatly increase.

Most Train Operating Companies will require you to complete the form online. However, there will still be a small number of companies that will send out paper-based forms; therefore, the content within this section has been created with both types of form in mind – online version and paper-based.

PREPARING TO COMPLETE THE APPLICATION FORM

Most of the sections on the application form are relatively straightforward to complete. However, there are a number of very important sections that will need your utmost attention if you are to succeed. First of all, read the following tips and advice that relate to the completion of your application form:

Read everything first

This applies to both the application form, the accompanying literature (if any) and the TOC website. You will need to understand a little bit about the company first before you can successfully complete the application form. You should also study the job description, person specification and the accompanying recruitment guidance notes.

Correct ink colour

Unless you are submitting an on-line application make sure you read any requirements that relate to ink colour or capital letters etc. The TOC Recruitment Office will receive many applications for every job advertised and the initial sift will look at minor errors such as these. If you cannot follow simple instructions, such as the correct ink colour, then there is not much chance you'll be able to check tickets properly! Read everything carefully and follow all of the instructions.

Complete a rough draft first

The first time around you are more than likely to make some mistakes. I advise that you photocopy the application form first (unless you are completing an on-line version) and complete a rough draft first. This will give you the opportunity to practice. Then, once you have finished your application, take a copy of it so that you can refer to it before you attend the interview. The interview panel will most certainly refer to your application form during the interview.

Before you complete the form you may get asked a number of questions to assess your eligibility for the role. Here are a few examples of the types of questions you might get asked:

EXAMPLES OF ELIGIBILITY QUESTIONS

Q. Do you have defective colour vision?

If you answer yes to this question it may hinder your ability to perform the role safely.

Q. Would you be willing to work unregular or unsociable shift patterns?

If you say no to this question, you will not pass the application form stage. Remember, one of the key qualities is that of flexibility.

Q. Do you currently live within a 60 minute commutable distance from your home to the location you are applying for?

If you live too far away from the location of work, it might be harder for you to get in to work and you may not get past the application form stage. Trains need to run on time and they cannot operate without a Train Conductor.

Q. Are you aged 18 or over?

The minimum age for this role is 18.

Q. Are there any restrictions to your residency in the UK which might affect your right to take up employment?

Q. If 'yes', please specify (UK Residency restrictions)

Q. If you are successful in your application, would you require a work permit prior to taking up employment?

Q. Do you have any convictions?

I often get asked by many people if their convictions will go against them when they apply. My answer is always this: you must be honest when you apply for the role. Put down any previous convictions on your application form and in accordance with the guidance notes. If you are unsure, contact the Train Operating Company to seek advice.

If yes, please give details.

Q. Do you have your own transport?

If you do not have you own transport how do you propose to get to work? If you plan on getting to work via public transport, what will you do if it gets delayed? Having your own reliable transport is the best option here.

Q. Are there any adjustments that may be required to be made should you be invited for interview?

Q. If the job demands it, are you willing to work shifts including nights, weekends and unsociable hours?

The answer here should always be YES!

On the following pages I have provided you with a number of sample responses to some of the more common types of application form question. The 'question and answer' sections on the application form are very important and represent an opportunity for you to show the recruitment staff at the TOC how good you are. Before each question I have explained what the question means and how best to construct your response to it. Then, I have provided a sample response to each question. Please note that these are to be used as a guide only. It is important that you answer the questions on your application form based on your own experiences and knowledge.

SAMPLE QUESTION NUMBER 1

Now that you've read more about the job, please tell us why you're applying for it and what knowledge, experience or skills you have that might be relevant.

The clue in this type of question is to READ about the job you are applying for. The question is asking you to match your knowledge, experience and skills with the job you have applied for. Therefore, you need to read the job description before responding. Job descriptions or person specifications usually have both 'essential' and 'desirable' criteria included. Basically you must provide evidence of where you can meet the 'essential' criteria on your application form. Desirable criteria will gain you extra marks but they are not essential.

If the TOC have not sent you a copy of the job description then try to obtain a copy of it before completing the form. This will give you an insight into the role that you are applying for. Once you have read the information about the post you will then be able to construct a suitable answer. Try to include any knowledge, skills or experience you may have that relates to the job description. If you have experience or knowledge in health and safety, working in pressurised situations or working in a customer-based environment then you may wish to include these also.

Now take a look at the following sample response before constructing your own, based on your own skills, knowledge and experience.

SAMPLE RESPONSE TO QUESTION NUMBER 1

I am applying for this post because I am looking for a new and challenging role. I enjoy working in a customer-focused environment and believe I would make an excellent Train Conductor for your company. I am also prepared to relocate to live within 60 minutes of the station. I understand that the company is changing and moving forward and I believe you would be an exciting company to work for. I also believe I can bring something to the team in terms of commitment, motivation, flexibility and enthusiasm.

I have worked in a customer-based role for a number of years now and during this time I have developed skills that can be applied to the role of a Train Conductor. As well as being a good communicator and possessing excellent organisational skills I am also highly safety-conscious and understand that this is a very important element of the role. In addition to my 12 years' experience in a customer-focused role I worked for 4 years with the Royal Navy. I am therefore a highly disciplined person and a very good team player. I have educational qualifications in English Language, English Literature and Art and I am also coming to the end of studying for a Diploma in Management Studies. I also hold a Health and Safety qualification through IODA in Nottingham. I am a fit and active person who visits the gym/swimming pool three times a week and I also play football for a local Sunday team. I am a very good communicator and learn new skills quickly. I am used to working long and varied hours and I understand that the role requires a high level of flexibility, which I am prepared for. I enjoy working with, and meeting people from all walks of life and I truly value the benefits of a diverse workforce. To summarise, I am a highly professional, caring, trustworthy, friendly and motivated person and I believe I would make an excellent member of the Train Operating Company team.

SAMPLE QUESTION NUMBER 2

Please tell us about anything you get up to outside work that gives us a better idea of what you're like as a person and why you might be right for our company. Please give the name of the activity and what it says about you.

This type of question is designed to assess the type of person you are outside of work. This will give the company an idea of how you are likely to perform at work and will tell them if you are fit, healthy and active. When responding to this type of question, make sure you make reference to the job description. What type of duties will you be required to perform and can you match your external activities to them? Being fit and active is always a positive aspect that the recruitment staff will be looking for. If you are active outside of work, then you are also likely to be active at work and achieve your tasks to the required standard. If you have recently achieved any educational or academic qualifications outside of work then it would be a good idea to make reference to these too. Now take a look at the sample response before creating your own based around your own skills, knowledge and experience.

SAMPLE RESPONSE TO QUESTION NUMBER 2

KEEPING FIT – I attend the gym at least 3 times per week and carry out some light weight work. Whilst at the gym, I usually perform 20 minutes of rowing each time and cover a distance of 5,000 metres. I particularly enjoy swimming and swim 50 lengths, 3 times per week. When I get the opportunity, I like to go walking, too, in order to keep healthy. Staying fit and healthy means that I am able to maintain a high level of concentration at work and it also helps to keep my enthusiasm and motivation levels high. This shows that I am a dedicated and determined person who is always looking to improve himself.

MUSICIAN – I currently play the drums and piano. I have always enjoyed being creative and I play the drums in a function band that plays at wedding events and parties on some weekends. This shows that I have the dedication to learn new skills and I have the ability to concentrate on the task in hand when required. Learning new skills is essential to the role of a Train Conductor and I believe that I have the ability to learn new skills quickly and adapt them to the work environment in a safe and effective manner.

SAMPLE QUESTION NUMBER 3

As the role you've applied for means that you'll be dealing with the safety of our customers and the delivery of our operation, we would like to hear examples of how you have used your initiative to solve a difficult problem.

Having the initiative to solve problems is integral to the Train Conductors role. On many occasions you will be on your own in the carriage and you will have to deal with sometimes difficult and challenging situations. Whilst you will have set procedures and guidelines to adhere to, you must still have the required initiative to solve difficult problems. Before responding to questions of this nature, make sure you READ the question first and try to understand what is required. Remember to write a response that identifies the use of your initiative to solve a difficult problem.

SAMPLE RESPONSE TO QUESTION NUMBER 3

During a recent staff meeting I was aware that there were a number of problems between some members of the team. The team wasn't working effectively so we all discussed ways in which we could improve. The actions of the team were starting to have an effect on the team's performance, so I decided to take the initiative to resolve the issue. I facilitated the meeting and asked everybody to share their views and opinions. I listened to each person individually and tried to encourage people to come up with solutions in order to improve the team's effectiveness. A positive point that came from our discussions was that people felt that we didn't hold enough meetings to talk about the problems we all face. It was agreed that with immediate effect we would hold weekly meetings to discuss issues, gather and share information, and look for ways that we could all support each other in our work. Since the meeting the team has moved forward and is now working far more effectively.

SAMPLE QUESTION NUMBER 4

As the role you've applied for means that you'll be dealing with the safety of our customers and the delivery of our operation, we would like to hear examples of how you have played a positive role as team member or leader.

Having the ability to work as an effective team member is important in any organisation and Train Operating Companies are no exception. The TOC will be made up of many different people, all of whom have an important role to perform. Therefore, it is essential that you have had some experience of working in a team environment, either as a team member or team leader. Try to think of an occasion when you have been part of a team or have even been the leader of a team. When responding to questions of this nature, think of a scenario where you worked as part of the team to achieve a task or solve a problem. Now take a look at the following sample response before using blank sheet of paper to construct your own.

SAMPLE RESPONSE TO QUESTION NUMBER 4

In my current role, I am responsible for the safety of my team and for ensuring that any health and safety incidents are reported in line with company regulations. I am also involved in coaching and mentoring my team and providing them with feedback, often helping them to improve. I currently lead a team of 18 staff and I am required to ensure the team operates effectively in terms of management, health and safety, and training. Following any incident that relates to health and safety I always fully brief each member of the team to ensure that I have done everything in my power to prevent an incident occurring again.

SAMPLE QUESTION NUMBER 5

As the role you've applied for means that you'll be dealing with the safety of our customers and the delivery of our operation, we would like to hear examples of how you have had to work under pressure.

If you are successful in your pursuit of becoming a Train Conductor, you will undoubtedly have to on occasions work under pressure. Maybe you will experience technical difficulties whilst on the train or the air conditioning will fail. It will be your responsibility to inform the passengers of the issues and keep them updated of delays or progress. You will undoubtedly be presented with scenarios and situations where you have to remain calm and focused and this question is designed to assess your ability to do just that. Try to think of a scenario where you have worked under pressure but still achieved the task or goal.

Take a look at the following sample response before using a blank sheet of paper to construct your own response based on your own experiences.

SAMPLE RESPONSE TO QUESTION NUMBER 5

In my current role as customer service manager I am required to work under pressure on a daily basis. Recently, I was presented with a situation where two members of staff had gone sick leaving me with only three other staff members to manage the shop during a busy Saturday.

During the morning we were due to take a stock delivery which meant that I had to perform many tasks without taking a break. During the day I dealt with two customer complaints, took delivery of the stock, served customers whilst others took their break and also dealt with a fire alarm actuation. I am often required to perform under pressure and thrive in such conditions. I always adapt well to situations like these and ensure that I still maintain a high level of professionalism at all times.

SAMPLE QUESTION NUMBER 6

As the role you've applied for means that you'll be dealing with the safety of our customers and the delivery of our operation, we would like to hear examples of how you have taken responsibility to communicate an important message.

As a Train Conductor you will have to communicate important messages to the customers. The messages may relate to the delayed departure or arrival of the train and these must be communicated sensitively. Try to think of an occasion where you have had to communicate an important message where you were under pressure. Take a look at the following sample response which will help you to create your own. Once you have read the provided example, use a blank sheet of paper to construct your own response based on your own experiences.

SAMPLE RESPONSE TO QUESTION NUMBER 6

Whilst working in my current position as a sales person I was the duty manager for the day as my manager had gone sick. It was the week before Christmas and the shop was very busy. During the day the fire alarm went off and I started to ask everybody to evacuate the shop, which is our company policy. The alarm has gone off in the past but the normal manager usually lets people stay in the shop whilst he finds out if it's a false alarm. This was a difficult situation because the shop was very busy, nobody wanted to leave, and my shop assistants were disagreeing with me in my decision to evacuate the shop. Some of the customers were becoming irate as they were in the changing rooms at the time. Both the customers and my shop assistants were disagreeing with me. The customers were saying that it was appalling that they had to evacuate the shop and that they would complain to the head office about it. My sales staff were trying to persuade me to keep everybody inside the shop and that it was most probably a false alarm, like it usually is. I was determined to evacuate everybody from the shop for safety reasons and would not allow anybody to deter me from my aim. The safety of my staff and customers was at the forefront of my mind, even though it wasn't at theirs. I persisted with my actions and eventually got everybody to leave the shop. When the Fire Service arrived they informed me that there had been a small fire at the rear of the shop and that the actions I had taken were the right ones. Everybody was safe and nobody was hurt as a result of the incident.

SAMPLE QUESTION NUMBER 7

Please give details of any personal development you have undertaken.

You may get asked this question on the application form as the role of a Train Conductor requires an ability to continually develop and learn new skills. Take a look at the following sample response which will help you to gain an understanding of what is required.

SAMPLE RESPONSE TO QUESTION NUMBER 7

Although I am in my late thirties I had always wanted to learn to play the guitar. It is something that I have wanted to do for many years, but have never had the time to learn until recently. One day I was watching a band play with my wife at my local pub and decided there and then that I would make it my mission to learn to play competently. The following day I went onto the internet and searched for a good guitar tutor in my local area. Luckily, I managed to find one within my town who had a very good reputation for teaching. I immediately booked a block of lessons and started my first one within a week. My development in the use of playing the guitar progressed rapidly and I soon achieved grade 1 standard. Every night of the week I would dedicate at least 30 minutes of time to my learning, in addition to my one hour weekly lesson. I soon found that I was progressing through the grades quickly, which was due to my level of learning commitment and a desire to become competent in playing the instrument. I recently achieved level 4 and I am now working to level 5 standard. I am also now playing in a local band and the opportunities for me, both musically and socially, have increased tenfold since learning to play. In addition to this, learning to play the guitar has improved my concentration levels and my patience. I am always looking to improve myself and I am very keen on continuous personal development.

SAMPLE QUESTION NUMBER 8

Please give an example of when you have provided excellent customer service.

It goes without saying that, in order to become a great Train Conductor, you will need to provide excellent customer service. As a Train Conductor you are a role model for the TOC and providing excellent service is very important if the organisation is to remain profitable. Take a look at the following sample response to this question.

SAMPLE RESPONSE TO QUESTION NUMBER 8

Whilst working as a shop assistant in my current role, a member of the public came in to complain about a pair of football shoes that he had bought for his son's birthday. When his son came to open the present on the morning of his birthday, he noticed that one of the football boots was a larger size than the other. He was supposed to be playing football with his friends that morning and wanted to wear his new boots. However, due to the shop's mistake, this was not possible. Naturally, the boy was very upset.

I remained calm throughout and listened to the gentleman very carefully, showing complete empathy for his son's situation. This immediately defused any potential confrontation. Once I had listened to his complaint I then told him how sorry I was for the mistake that had happened, and that I would feel exactly the same if it was my own son who it had happened to. I then told the gentleman that I would refund the money in full and give his son a new pair of football boots to the same value as the previous pair.

The man was delighted with my offer and resolution to the complaint. Not only that, I then offered to give the man a further discount of 10% on any future purchase, due to the added inconvenience that was caused by him having to return to the shop to sort out the problem. I believe customer service is very important in any work-related role, as it is the customer that keeps the business profitable. The potential for losing a customer was averted by my actions and I felt sure the man would return to our shop again.

SAMPLE QUESTION NUMBER 9

Please give details of when you have dealt with a difficult situation.

As a Train Conductor you will be required to take responsibility for dealing with difficult situations. It might be a rude passenger who is under the influence of alcohol or drugs, or you may come across a passenger who is feeling ill. This question is designed to see whether or not you have any experience of taking responsibility for difficult situations and, more importantly, resolving them.

SAMPLE RESPONSE TO QUESTION NUMBER 9

One evening I was sat at home watching television when I heard my next door neighbours smoke alarm sounding. This is not an unusual occurrence as she is always setting off the alarm whilst cooking. However, on this occasion, something was different as the alarm did not normally sound so late at night. I got up out of my chair and went to see if she was OK. She is a vulnerable, elderly lady and I always look out for her whenever possible. When I arrived next door I peered through the window and noticed my neighbour sat asleep on the chair in the front room. Wisps of smoke were coming from the kitchen so I knew that she was in trouble. I immediately ran back into my house and dialled 999 calmly. I asked for the Fire Service and the Ambulance Service and explained that a person was stuck inside the house with a fire burning in the kitchen. I provided the call operator as much information as possible including landmarks close to our road to make it easier for the Fire Service to find. As soon as I got off the phone I immediately went round the back of my house to climb over the fence. Mrs Watson, my neighbour, usually leaves her back door unlocked until she goes to bed. I climbed over the fence and tried the door handle. Thankfully the door opened. I entered into the kitchen and turned off the gas heat which was burning dried up soup. I then ran to the front room, woke up Mrs Watson and carried her carefully through the front door, as this was the nearest exit. I then sat Mrs Watson down on the pavement outside and placed my coat around her. It wasn't long before the Fire Service arrived and they took over from them on in. I gave them all of the details relating to the incident and informed them of my actions when in the kitchen.

SAMPLE QUESTION NUMBER 10

Please give details of when your communications skills made a difference to a situation.

Being able to communicate effectively is crucial to the role of a Train Conductor. Not only will you have to speak face-to-face with many passengers each day during your shift, but you will also have to give announcements on the PA system as well as speaking directly with the train driver. Take a look at the following sample response to this question.

SAMPLE RESPONSE TO QUESTION NUMBER 10

My next door neighbour had a cat they had looked after for years and they were very fond of it. I had to inform them that their cat had just been run over by a car in the road. I was fully aware of how much they loved their cat and I could understand that the message I was about to tell them would have been deeply distressing. They had cherished the cat for years and to suddenly lose it would have been a great shock to them. To begin with I knocked at their door and ask calmly if I could come in to speak to them. Before I broke the news to them I made them a cup of tea and sat them down in a quiet room away from any distractions. I then carefully and sensitively told them that their cat had passed away following an accident in the road. At all times I took into account their feelings and I made sure I delivered the message sensitively and in a caring manner. I took into account where and when I was going to deliver the message. It was important to tell them in a quiet room away from any distractions so that they could grieve in peace. I also took into account the tone in which I delivered the message and I also made sure that I was sensitive to their feelings. I also made sure that I would be available to support them after I had broken the news. I strongly believe that the manner in which I communicated and delivered the message was helpful to the already difficult situation.

FINAL TIPS FOR CREATING A SUCCESSFUL APPLICATION FORM

- Read the form carefully before starting to complete it. Also be sure to read all of the accompanying guidance notes, person specification and job description.

- Follow all instructions carefully. Your form can be rejected for failing to follow simple instructions.

- If you are completing a handwritten version of the form make sure your handwriting is neat, legible, concise and grammatically correct. You will lose marks for incorrect spelling!

- Before you submit the form get somebody to check over it for you.

- Once you have completed the form make sure you make a photocopy of it. You may be asked questions that relate to your responses during the interview.

- Send the form recorded delivery if completing a paper-based version. I have known of many application forms to go missing in the post.

CHAPTER FIVE

THE ASSESSMENT CENTRE

If you are invited to attend the assessment centre, it will normally follow around one week after the selection interview. I have purposely placed the assessment centre section before the interview as I feel it is a more natural way to progress through this guide. Details relating to the interview will be provided during a later chapter.

The assessment centre is designed specifically to help the Train Operating Company select the best people for the job. You will be asked to sit a number of paper-and-pencil exercises and undertake a structured interview. During the assessment centre the TOC will further assess your ability to succeed in the job. In particular they will be looking at your ability to deal with ticket checks/sales, your concentration skills and your ability to deal with unexpected situations. People who do well at the assessment centre tend to do well in the Conductor role itself.

Within this section I have provided you with some sample test questions and also tips on preparing for the assessment centre.

When you attend the assessment centre, there are a few basic rules that you need to adhere to. If the TOC state on the welcoming letter that you should provide passport size photographs, be sure to take along the required number and also any additional items of identification they request. If you do not have the requested ID then you may not be permitted to sit the assessment centre. I also strongly advise you dress smartly/formally for the assessment centre. This means a smart, clean, pressed suit for the gentleman and a blouse, skirt or trousers for the ladies.

ON ARRIVAL AT THE ASSESSMENT CENTRE

When you arrive at the centre the centre manager or assessment centre administrator will check your forms of identification and also take any pictures they requested off you before confirming your name and address etc. They will then usually split you up into groups, if there are a large number of applicants.

The room where you will be taking the assessments will be set up like a classroom with tables and chairs. This is the room where you will sit the paper-based exams/tests. They will ask everyone to switch off all mobile phones and pagers and to also remove your jackets and coats. You will also be asked if you are fit and able to undertake the tests.

You will then normally be supplied with spare paper to do any working outs on and also a rubber, pen or pencil in order to complete the assessments with. For your comfort you will also be supplied with a glass or bottle of water for you to

 how2become

drink if you wish. The administrator will then go into detail and explain what will be happening during the assessment centre and also the usual health and safety requirements.

They may also tell you that after each test they will mark your answers and those who don't meet the required standard will be asked to leave. Those who are successful will be re-admitted for the afternoon session whilst those who are not will be debriefed and informed to reapply after 6 months.

The afternoon session will usually include an interview with either the centre administrator and/or a train crew manager.

DOCUMENT SALES TEST

Part of the process of applying to become a Train Conductor means that you will have to sit a number of different assessments. One of the tests you will be required to undertake is an assessment that measures your levels of decision making and accuracy. This is usually done by undertaking an assessment that focuses on your ability to sell tickets correctly; one of the many duties you will be expected to undertake as a Train Conductor.

Within this section, we have provided you with 60 practice questions that you can use to improve your decision making and accuracy skills, which you can then apply to your real assessment.

Please note, in your real Train Conductor assessment, you will only need to answer 30 questions in approximately 18 minutes. We have provided you with additional questions in order to improve your performance and enhance your skills in this particular area of testing. It is unlikely that you will be able to finish the questions in the time frame provided, therefore it is important that you work through the questions quickly and

effectively. You will LOSE marks for any incorrect answers, so we strongly recommend that you focus on accuracy as well as speed, and avoid any wild or panic guessing.

However, we cannot stress enough that the practice sample test within this guide, is merely a test designed to assess the same skills required to pass the ACTUAL assessment. The sample test DOES NOT reflect the same contents of the actual test, and therefore should not be used as anything more than a practice tool to improve your skills and competencies to become a Train Conductor.

Within this practice test, you will be provided with 4 sources which will highlight the key information that you will need to refer to in regards to ticket prices of a theme park. The test will require you to process the information in the 4 tables and answer the questions relating to change and cost.

Answer the following 60 questions in 40 minutes.

EXAMPLE

Using the source cards (found on the next couple of pages), you will have to determine the correct cost of the tickets based on the information within these source card tables.

So, you may be given a question like so:

A group of three adults and three children arrive at the gates of the theme park and wish to purchase their tickets. They arrive during off peak hours, and would like to purchase tickets for the ultimate fast track. How much will this cost them in total?

The next step, is to determine which source card you need to use. You should notice that you need to use the table for 'Off

Peak Fast Track' (the one shown below).

Off Peak Fast Track			
	Child	**Adult**	**Senior**
Ultimate Fast Track	£40.99	£68.99	£56.00
Extreme Fast Track	£39.99	£57.99	£40.00
Hydro Fast Track	£25.99	£45.99	£37.00
Mini Fast Track	£8.99	£15.00	£10.00

* *On peak fast track is 5% more than off peak fast track.*

You will then need to add up all of the prices per ticket to find out the overall total.

$(68.99 \times 3) + (40.99 \times 3) =$

$(206.97) + (122.97) =$

329.94

Therefore, the customers would need to pay £329.94

REMEMBER – *for these types of questions you need to pay attention to what the table is showing you. As shown in the above table, this is for off-peak hours. So if you needed to work out the on-peak hours, you would need to read the statement marked with the asterisk (*) to see what the cost of the tickets would be.*

Now you have a clearer understanding of how to tackle these types of questions, work through the 60 practice questions, and see how well you get on.

how2become

SOURCE CARDS

On Peak Gate Tickets			
	Child	Adult	Senior
1 Day Ticket	£25.99	£48.99	£36.00
2 Day Ticket	£49.99	£87.99	£50.00
Group Ticket (10 or more)	£15.99 pp	£35.99 pp	£27.00 pp

Total cost booked online in advance, is 15% less than total of gate fares.

Off Peak Gate Tickets			
	Child	Adult	Senior
1 Day Ticket	£18.99	£39.99	£29.00
2 Day Ticket	£35.99	£72.99	£45.00
Group Ticket (10 or more)	£11.99 pp	£28.99 pp	£20.00 pp

Total cost booked online in advance, is 15% less than total of gate fares.

Off Peak Fast Track			
	Child	Adult	Senior
Ultimate Fast Track	£40.99	£68.99	£56.00
Extreme Fast Track	£39.99	£57.99	£40.00
Hydro Fast Track	£25.99	£45.99	£37.00
Mini Fast Track	£8.99	£15.00	£10.00

On peak fast track is 5% more than off peak fast track.

Accommodation		
Child (12 under)	**Adult**	**Senior**
1 night	Free	£34.00	£25.00
2 nights	Free	£58.99	£40.00
3 nights	Free	£75.99	£57.00
4 nights	Free	£96.00	£75.00

* Any more nights after 4, will cost the nights of 4 plus 25% of the price for one more night. Prices are per person.

DOCUMENT SALES TEST

Question 1
Two adults want to purchase off-peak ultimate fast track tickets. How much will the customers need to give you?

Answer [　　　　　　　]

Question 2
One adult and one child pay for the 1 day off-peak tickets. How much will you need to be given?

Answer [　　　　　　　]

Question 3
A customer books online for five adults during off-peak hours for the 1 day tickets. How much will you need to be given?

Answer [　　　　　　　]

Question 4
Three children and two adults come to the theme park and purchase on-peak 2 day tickets. How much will it cost them?

Answer [　　　　　　　]

Question 5
A hen party has arrived at the theme park and wants to book for a group of ten adults. They have arrived at peak time. They want the cheapest tickets. Calculate the total cost for the group which would be the best price for them.

Answer [　　　　　　　]

Question 6
Two children, one adult and one senior book in advance for the 1 day off-peak tickets. How much would they have to pay in total?

Answer

Question 7
Two adults want to buy extreme fast track tickets on peak time. They give you £130. How much change do you need to give them?

Answer

Question 8
Two adults pay in advance for the 1 day off-peak tickets. They wish to stay at the theme park for 1 night. In total, how much will it cost them for their tickets and accommodation?

Answer

Question 9
Four children are accompanied by three adults and wish to purchase off-peak mini fast track tickets. How much change will you need to give them if they give you £90?

Answer

Question 10
One child and four adults have booked in advance for the on-peak 2 day tickets. What is their total cost?

Answer

Question 11

How much would it cost a group of ten people including six children and four adults for off-peak time?

Answer [   ]

Question 12

A family of two children and two adults have arrived at the theme park and want to find out the best possible price. They are told about a special offer that allows children to go half price. They wish to purchase the ultimate fast track tickets for off-peak time. How much will they pay if they take up the special offer?

Answer [   ]

Question 13

Five adults want to book the 2 day on-peak tickets at the gate, and pay for 2 nights in accommodation. How much will each person pay if they were to split the cost equally?

Answer [   ]

Question 14

What is the difference in price for the 2 day off-peak gate ticket for a child, compared to the 2 day off-peak gate ticket for an adult?

Answer [   ]

Question 15
Seven adults and four children wish to book for the hydro fast track option during peak time. How much change will you need to give them if they give you £460?

Answer

Question 16
How much would it cost one adult and one child if they booked online for the 2 day tickets during peak hours?

Answer

Question 17
How much would it cost one adult for a ticket during on-peak hours for the extreme fast track ticket?

Answer

Question 18
Three adults and two children arrive during off-peak hours and want to purchase the 1 day tickets. They want to pay £65 of the cost on their credit card. How much will they need to give you in cash?

Answer

Question 19
How much would the customer save if they bought a 2 day adult ticket for on-peak hours, as opposed to buying two individual 1 day tickets for on-peak hours?

Answer

Question 20

How much would it cost two seniors, two adults and three children if they arrived off-peak and booked at the gates?

Answer

Question 21

Three adults for off-peak hours want to purchase tickets for the hydro fast track. One of the adults has a disability, and gets a 25% reduction for his individual ticket. How much will the group pay in total, including the reduction of the individual ticket?

Answer

Question 22

Five adults have booked online for a 2 day ticket during off-peak hours. How much will each person pay?

Answer

Question 23

What is the difference in price for an off-peak adult ultimate fast track, and an adult off-peak hydro fast track ticket?

Answer

Question 24

What is the difference in price for an on-peak adult extreme fast track ticket, and an on-peak ultimate fast track ticket?

Answer

Question 25

Within the school holidays, children get a 60% off discount pp. If a family of three adults and four children purchase tickets for off-peak times for the 2 day ticket, how much would it cost in total?

Answer

Question 26

What is the difference in price for an adult off-peak day ticket, compared with an adult off-peak ultimate fast track ticket?

Answer

Question 27

A couple wants to know how much it would cost them for 4 nights in accommodation, and the 2 day tickets for on-peak hours. They will be paying when they arrive there.

Answer

Question 28

Three adults wants to book gate tickets during on-peak hours. How much change would they receive if they wanted to book for the 1 day tickets and gave you £150?

Answer

Question 29

Six adults wish to book off-peak for fast track tickets. Two of them want to book for extreme fast track, whereas the other four adults wish to book for the ultimate fast track. How much would it cost the group in total?

Answer

Question 30

A group of thirteen people attend the theme park for a birthday celebration. They book using the group deal and book during peak hours. They book in advance. They are all paying for an adult ticket. How much will the total cost be for the entire group?

Answer

Question 31

How much would it cost in total if three children wanted the hydro fast track, and five adults wanted the extreme fast track, all for peak hours and bought at the gates?

Answer

Question 32

A group of eight children and three adults arrive at the theme park for off-peak hours. They wish to purchase the best deal. Find the best deal and work out the total cost.

Answer

Question 33

For a limited time only, the fast track tickets have all been discounted by 20% pp. Two adults and three children arrive in time for this offer. They wish to all purchase mini fast track tickets for peak hours. How much will it cost in total, taking into consideration this limited offer?

Answer

Question 34

Four adults pay for on-peak ultimate fast track tickets. They wish to pay £110 on card, and pay the rest by cash. How much cash would they need to give you?

Answer

Question 35

A child and a senior wish to pay for the 2 day tickets for off-peak hours and include 5 nights in accommodation. How much will need to be paid in order to cover all of the costs?

Answer

Question 36

Two adults wants to purchase the 2 day tickets for peak hours. They also want 7 night's accommodation. How much is the total cost?

Answer

Question 37

A customer wants a discount for not being able to park in the theme park car park. You offer them a 10% discount on the total cost. He wishes to pay for two adult tickets and four children tickets for peak times. How much will it cost him after this discount?

Answer

Question 38

A customer wants to know what the best price would be during peak hours for five tickets for the hydro fast track. Calculate the best price you could give him.

Answer

Question 39

A customer is enquiring how much extra they would have to pay if they wanted to stay 3 nights in accommodation for two adults and two children.

Answer

Question 40

How much would it cost for a family of two seniors, two adults and three children to spend two nights at the theme park?

Answer

Question 41

The theme park is now offering family discounts which comprise of two adults and two children. If a family wishes to use the family discount, they will receive 60% off standard tickets per person. How much would it cost a family if they wished to purchase 1 day tickets for on-peak hours?

Answer _____

Question 42

Six adults wish to purchase ultimate fast track tickets for on-peak hours. How much change would you need to give them if they gave you £500?

Answer _____

Question 43

A group of friends book online for five adult tickets and three children tickets for off-peak hours. How much will the group need to pay in total?

Answer _____

Question 44

What is the average cost across the prices for one child, one adult and one senior ticket for a 1 day pass during off-peak hours?

Answer _____

Question 45

Two adults, one senior and one adult wish to purchase off-peak gate tickets for 1 day at the theme park. The price for the senior ticket is deducted by 70% because of a disability card that they hold. How much would the group pay?

Answer

Question 46

Five friends have arrived at the theme park and want to purchase off-peak fast track tickets. Two of them want to purchase the hydro fast track, and the other three wish to purchase the extreme fast track tickets. They decide to just split the total cost equally. How much per person will each person need to pay?

Answer

Question 47

Three adults pay for the 2 day tickets for on-peak hours. You realise that they have only given you £225.00. How much money are they short of paying the full amount?

Answer

Question 48

A group of eighteen need to purchase their tickets at the gates. They want to book for off-peak tickets, and are all classed as adults. They wish to split the cost equally. How much will then need to pay per person?

Answer

Question 49

What is the difference in price for the 2 day ticket purchased at the gates during peak hours, compared to the 2 day ticket purchased at the gates during off-peak hours?

Answer

Question 50

What is the difference between the prices per ticket for a group adult ticket for off-peak hours, compared to that of on-peak hours?

Answer

Question 51

A school class arrives at the theme park on peak time for their school trip. The school received 30% off the total cost for booking a large group of twenty students and eight adults, plus another 15% off for booking online. How much did they pay in total?

Answer

Question 52

What is the difference in price for a child ultimate fast track ticket and an adult ultimate fast track ticket, both for off-peak hours?

Answer

Question 53

One adult pays for an on-peak hydro fast track ticket. How much will he have to pay?

Answer

Question 54

Five adults pay in advance for the 2 day tickets for on-peak hours. When they arrive at the theme park, they also wish to book 3 nights in accommodation. How much will it cost in total?

Answer

Question 55

An adult customer wants to know how much extra it will cost per night after staying 4 nights?

Answer

Question 56

A group of ten people ask you what the best price is to pay for off-peak gate tickets for six children, and four adults. Work out the best price you can offer the group.

Answer

Question 57

A recent discount has been implemented during the summer holidays. This discount will deduct 35% off the total price of accommodation only. A customer wishes to book for 2 nights for two adults, and pay for the 2 day tickets for on-peak hours. How much will she have to pay altogether?

Answer

Question 58

All fast track tickets have a discount of 10% per person. Four adults want to purchase extreme fast track tickets for off-peak hours. How much will they pay in total?

Answer

Question 59

What is the difference in price for the 1 day ticket for on-peak hours bought at the gates, and the 1 day ticket for on-peak hours bought online? (Both for an adult ticket).

Answer

Question 60

For one day only, the first twenty customers will receive a discount whereby children will go in for £1. The twentieth customer of the day arrives at the ticket booth, and asks for five children tickets and two adult tickets for off-peak hours. How much will it cost?

Answer

ANSWERS TO DOCUMENT SALES TEST

Q1. £137.98

Q2. £58.98

Q3. £169.96

Q4. £325.95

Q5. £359.90

Q6. £90.93

Q7. £8.24

Q8. £135.99

Q9. £9.04

Q10. £341.66

Q11. £187.90

Q12. £178.96

Q13. £146.98

Q14. £37.00

Q15. £12.92

Q16. £117.29

Q17. £60.88

Q18. £92.95

Q19. £9.99

Q20. £194.95

Q21. £126.48

Q22. £62.04

Q23. £23.00

Q24. £11.55

Q25. £276.57

Q26. £29.00

Q27. £367.98

Q28. £3.03

Q29. £391.94

Q30. £397.69

Q31. £386.24

Q32. £182.89

Q33. £47.85

Q34. £179.72

Q35. £162.24

Q36. £418.98

Q37. £181.75

Q38. £241.40

Q39. £151.98

Q40. £197.98

Q41. £60.00

Q42. £65.42

Q43. £218.39

Q44. £29.32

Q45. £107.67

Q46. £53.19

Q47. £38.97

Q48. £28.99

Q49. £15.00

Q50. £7.00

Q51. £334.25

Q52. £28.00

Q53. £48.28

Q54. £753.91

Q55. £8.50

Q56. £187.90

Q57. £252.67

Q58. £208.80

Q59. £7.34

Q60. £84.98

DOCUMENT AUDIT TEST

Another type of assessment that you will be required to undertake is that of a checking exam. Generally, this assessment will work alongside the previous sales test in order to gain an overall understanding of a candidate's ability to process information and make accurate decisions.

As a Train Conductor, you will be expected to move along the train and check passenger tickets as you go. Unlike the previous test which required you to sell the correct tickets, this assessment will assess whether you are capable of viewing tickets accurately to make sure they are valid. The duty of checking tickets is a crucial role to the job, therefore you need to demonstrate strong levels of competency. The Train Operating Company that you are applying for want to ensure themselves with employees who are able to prevent ticket fraud; an issue which costs the company millions of pounds every year. It is your duty to make sure that passengers are travelling with the correct ticket in order to comply with company standards.

Within this section, we have provided you with 60 practice questions that can be used to improve your ability regarding decision making and visual accuracy, which you can then apply to your real assessment.

Please note, in your real Train Conductor assessment, you will only need to answer 30 questions in approximately 12 minutes. We have provided you with additional questions in order to improve your performance and enhance your skills in this particular area of testing. It is unlikely that you will be able to finish the questions in the time frame provided, therefore it is important that you work through the questions quickly and effectively. You will LOSE marks for any incorrect answers,

so we strongly recommend that you focus on accuracy as well as speed, and avoid any wild or panic guessing.

However, we cannot stress enough that the practice sample test within this guide, is merely a test designed to assess the same skills required to pass the ACTUAL assessment. The sample test DOES NOT reflect the contents of the actual test, and therefore should not be used as anything more than a practice tool to improve your skills and competencies to become a Train Conductor.

Within the practice test, for each question you will be shown a receipt. You will need to determine whether that receipt is accurate based on the information provided. The test will require you to look at five areas which need to be checked to determine the receipt's accuracy:

- Date;

- Age (child, adult or senior);

- Times (on or off peak);

- Type of ticket (1 day, 2 day, group or fast track);

- Payment (gate ticket or advanced booking);

Please look at the examples below to highlight what the test will involve:

EXAMPLE

You are working at a theme park. Your job is to process customer's entrances and hand them a receipt.

Four adults arrive at the theme park on the 01.06.13 and working out which tickets to buy. They decide to opt for four ultimate fast track tickets. They arrive just after off-peak hours. They come up to you and ask for four adult tickets for the ultimate fast track.

You will then be shown the receipt of their purchase.

RECEIPT 1

4 x adult, off-peak, ultimate fast, gate ticket

Dated 01.06.13

You have five options to work against to check whether or not the information on the receipt is correct, according to the description of the purchase:

- Date (date of ticket purchased);

- Age (child, adult, senior);

- Time (on or off-peak);

- Type of ticket (one day, two day, group, fast track);

- Payment (gate ticket, paid in advance).

You will then be given a question similar to the following:

Is the receipt correct?

Answer – the ticket IS NOT correct

Date – yes, the date is the same;

Age – yes, the ticket shows four adult tickets, which is what the customers asked for;

Time – no, the customers arrive after off-peak hours, which means they arrive during peak hours;

Type – yes, they wished to purchase ultimate fast track tickets;

Payment – yes, they arrived at the gates and purchased their tickets there.

REMEMBER – *it only takes one of the five options to be incorrect for the receipt to be considered incorrect.*

Now that you have some understanding of what you can expect in this section, answer the following 60 questions in 25 minutes.

DOCUMENT AUDIT TEST

Question 1

Two adults have just arrived at the theme park on the 28.08.14 during peak hours. They have just bought two 1 day tickets for two adults. You give them their receipt.

> **RECEIPT**
>
> 2 x adults, on-peak, 1 day gate ticket
>
> Dated 28.08.14

Is their receipt correct?

Question 2

You have just served an adult and a child on the 07.06.13. The customers arrived during off-peak hours and purchased the 2 day tickets. You hand them their receipt of proof of payment.

> **RECEIPT**
>
> 1 x adult, off-peak, 1 day gate ticket
> 1 x child, off-peak, 1 day gate ticket
>
> Dated 07.06.13

Have they received the correct receipt details?

Question 3

One adult arrives during peak hours and purchases an ultimate fast track ticket. This ticket is only valid for the 22.04.13.

RECEIPT

1 x child, on-peak, ultimate fast track, gate ticket

Dated 22.04.13

Is the receipt accurate?

Question 4

Two adults and two children just purchase the hydro fast track ticket which they paid for online. They have arrived during peak hours of the theme park. You note that the date is 01.08.14. You read their confirmation email letter with proof of purchase and hand them their final receipt.

RECEIPT

2 x adults, on-peak, hydro fast, advance book

2 x child, on-peak, hydro fast, advance book

Dated 01.08.14

Is their receipt correct?

Question 5

Five adults have arrived at the theme park gates and purchase the extreme fast track tickets. They arrive during off-peak hours on the 25.07.13. They make their payment, and you hand them back their receipt.

RECEIPT

5 x adults, off-peak, extreme fast, gate ticket

Dated 25.07.13

Is the receipt accurate?

Question 6

Two adults and three children purchase tickets when they arrive at the gate. They have purchased the 1 day tickets for on peak hours. The date they arrive is the 06.05.11.

RECEIPT

2 x adults, on-peak, 2 day gate ticket

2 x child, on-peak, 2 day gate ticket

Dated 06.05.11

Is the information on the customers receipt correct?

Question 7

A group of six children and four adults arrive at the theme park on the 11.06.14 and purchase their group ticket when they arrive. They are charged the prices for off-peak hours.

RECEIPT

4 x adults, off-peak, group gate ticket

6 x child, off-peak, group gate ticket

                                        Dated 11.06.14

Is this receipt correct?

Question 8

Two adults arrive at the theme park and show their confirmation letter that they have booked online. They made their payments for the date 09.08.10. They purchased a 1 day ticket during peak hours. You read their confirmation letter, and print them a final receipt.

RECEIPT

2 x adults, on-peak, 2 day gate ticket, advance book

                                        Dated 08.09.10

Have you printed the correct receipt?

Question 9

Five adults arrive at the theme park and wish to purchase fast track tickets just for the hydro. You notice that the time is 5 minutes after off-peak time. The date is 08.06.12. You put their transaction through, and give them their receipt.

RECEIPT

5 x adults, off-peak, hydro fast, gate ticket

Dated 08.06.12

Is the receipt accurate of the proof of purchase?

Question 10

One adult, one senior and two children arrive at the park with an advanced booking for today's date of 05.04.14. They have paid for off-peak hours for a 1 day ticket, which they arrive in time for.

RECEIPT

1 x adult, off-peak, 1 day ticket, gate ticket
1 x senior, off-peak, 1 day ticket, gate ticket
1 x child, off-peak, 1 day ticket, gate ticket

Dated 05.04.13

Is the receipt correct?

Question 11

Three adults wish to purchase tickets at the gates for the ultimate fast track option. The date is 10.09.10 and will be paying for on-peak hours. You process their transaction, and give them a receipt.

> **RECEIPT**
>
> 3 x child, on-peak, extreme fast, gate ticket
>
>   Dated 11.05.14

Is the receipt accurate?

Question 12

Two seniors and two children arrive at the theme park. They have booked in advance for off-peak 1 day tickets for the date of 04.03.11.

> **RECEIPT**
>
> 1 x senior, on-peak, 1 day ticket, advance book
> 1 x child, on-peak, 1 day ticket, advance book
>
>   Dated 05.03.11

Is the customers receipt correct?

Question 13

Six adults wish to purchase the ultimate fast track tickets. They have not made any advanced bookings. They arrive just in time to book for off-peak hours. You sell them their tickets, and hand over a receipt for proof of purchase. The date is 11.06.13.

RECEIPT

6 x adults, off-peak, ultimate fast, gate ticket

Dated 11.06.14

Is the receipt correct?

Question 14

Five children and two adults arrive at the theme park on the 15.06.14. They wish to purchase the 2 day tickets, for on-peak hours.

RECEIPT

2 x adults, on-peak, 2 day ticket, gate ticket
5 x child, on-peak, 2 day ticket, gate ticket

Dated 15.06.14

Does the receipt contain the correct information?

 how2become

Question 15

Eleven adults arrive at the theme park with an advanced booking for just one day at the park during on-peak hours. They arrive on scheduled date for 17.05.08

> **RECEIPT**
>
> 11 x adults, on-peak, group ticket, advance book
>
> Dated 15.05.08

Is the receipt correct?

Question 16

Four adults arrive at the park and need to purchase tickets for off peak hours on the 18.06.14. They wish to pay for two adults together, and then pay for the other two. You put their transactions through separately, and give them two receipts for proof of purchase. They all want to book for the hydro fast track.

> **RECEIPT 1**
>
> 2 x adults, off-peak, 1 day gate ticket
>
> Dated 18.06.14

> **RECEIPT 2**
>
> 2 x adults, off-peak, 1 day gate ticket
>
> Dated 18.06.14

Are both of the receipts correct?

Question 17

A family of two adults and two children arrive at the theme park already having a booking. They arrive on the scheduled date of 13.05.11, during peak hours. They are only there for 1 day.

> **RECEIPT**
>
> 2 x adults, on-peak, 1 day ticket, gate ticket
> 2 x child, on-peak, 1 day ticket, gate ticket
>
>   Dated 13.05.11

Is this receipt correct?

Question 18

Four adults arrive at the theme park and want to book for the 2 day tickets during on-peak hours. They want to book so that day 1 is today which is the 09.07.12.

> **RECEIPT**
>
> 4 x adults, on-peak, 2 day ticket, gate ticket
>
>   Dated 09.07.12

Is the receipt correct?

Question 19

Three adults and five children want to book for the extreme fast track option for the 19.05.10. They come during off-peak hours.

> **RECEIPT**
>
> 5 x adults, off-peak, extreme fast, gate ticket
> 3 x child, off-peak, extreme fast, gate ticket
>
> Dated 19.06.10

Is the receipt accurate?

Question 20

You are the ticket sales person at a theme park, whose job it is to process customer's entrances and hand them their receipt. Three children wish to pay for the 1 day ticket for off-peak hours on the 17.08.14.

> **RECEIPT**
>
> 3 x child, off-peak, 1 day gate ticket
>
> Dated 17.08.14

Is the receipt correct?

 how2become

Question 21

Two seniors and three children have booked in advanced for a 1 day ticket on the 23.08.13. They have booked for on-peak hours. They arrive at the theme park and hand you their confirmation letter that they received via email. You process this information, and hand them a receipt.

> **RECEIPT**
>
> 2 x seniors, on-peak, 1 day ticket, advance book
> 3 x child, on-peak, 1 day ticket, advance book
>
> Dated 23.08.13

Is this receipt correct?

Question 22

A group of sixteen adults have booked in advance for the 22.05.11. They arrive at the theme park on this day, and want to book for on-peak hours. They wish to pay in two instalments. They want to pay for 6 people together, then the rest of the group. You put both transactions receipt and hand back the group two receipts.

> **RECEIPT 1**
>
> 6 x adults, on-peak, group ticket, gate ticket
>
> Dated 22.05.11

> **RECEIPT 2**
>
> 11 x adults, on-peak, group ticket, gate ticket
>
> Dated 22.05.11

Are both receipts accurate?

Question 23

Seven adults arrive at the park and want to purchase the 2 day ticket for off-peak hours for just the day. They arrive on the 07.08.10. They are all paying together. You print off their receipt and hand it to them.

RECEIPT

7 x adults, on-peak, 2 day ticket, gate ticket

Dated 07.08.10

Does the receipt contain the correct details?

Question 24

Four adults and six children arrive at theme park having already booked for the 2 day ticket commencing on today's date of 04.09.11. They have booked these tickets for off-peak hours.

RECEIPT

4 x adults, off-peak, 2 day ticket, advance book
6 x child, off-peak, 2 day ticket, advance book

Dated 04.09.11

Is the receipt correct?

Question 25

One adult wishes to purchase an ultimate fast track ticket for on-peak hours for the 07.07.12. He pays at the gate.

RECEIPT

1 x adults, on-peak, ultimate fast, gate ticket

Dated 07.07.12

Is the receipt accurate?

Question 26

Five children, two adults and one senior arrive at the gates of the theme park, and they need to purchase their tickets. They decide to pay for everyone to have mini fast track tickets. The date of arrival of these customers is the 09.05.08, and have arrived 5 minutes late from when the off-peak hours ended.

RECEIPT

2 x adults, off-peak, mini fast, advance book
5 x child, off-peak, mini fast, advance book
1 x senior, off-peak, mini fast, advance book

Dated 09.05.08

Is the receipt correct?

Question 27

Three seniors and three adults arrive at the theme park on the 20.06.09. They have booked in advance for off-peak tickets for just one day at the park.

> **RECEIPT**
>
> 3 x adults, off-peak, 1 day ticket, advance book
> 3 x seniors, off-peak, 1 day ticket, advance book
>
> Dated 20.06.09

Is the receipt correct?

Question 28

A family of three children and two adults have booked in advance. They have all purchased extreme fast track tickets during off-peak hours. Their booking is scheduled for 16.08.14, which is todays date.

> **RECEIPT**
>
> 2 x adults, off-peak, extreme fast, advance book
> 3 x child, off-peak, extreme fast, advance book
>
> Dated 16.08.14

Is the receipt correct?

Question 29

A group of eight friends arrive at the theme park and want to purchase fast track tickets. They are all classed as adults. Four of them want the ultimate fast track, whereas the other four want the hydro fast track. They are happy to pay together. The date is the 28.07.13, and it is 5 minutes into peak hours.

RECEIPT

4 x adults, on-peak, ultimate fast, gate ticket
4 x adults, on-peak, hydro fast, gate ticket

Dated 28.07.13

Is this receipt accurate?

Question 30

Two families arrive together, and wish to purchase the 2 day tickets. Each family comprises of two adults and two children. They arrive on the 18.06.10 during off-peak hours, and would like to pay separately. You tell them that you will put the transaction through separately so that they can each pay for their own family. You hand them back two receipts.

RECEIPT 1

2 x adults, off-peak, 2 day ticket, gate ticket
2 x child, off-peak, 2 day ticket, gate ticket

Dated 18.06.10

RECEIPT 2

2 x adults, off-peak, 1 day ticket, gate ticket
2 x child, off-peak, 1 day ticket, gate ticket

Dated 18.06.10

Are both of these receipts valid?

 how2become

Question 31

A group of twelve children and five adults arrive at the theme park for a school trip. They have booked in advance for the date of 10.03.13, during peak hours. They have purchased a group ticket.

> **RECEIPT**
>
> 5 x adults, off-peak, group ticket, advance book
> 12 x child, off-peak, group ticket, advance book
>
> Dated 10.03.13

Is the receipt correct?

Question 32

You have just arrived at your job which is 10 minutes after off-peak hours ended. You serve the next customer. A family of two adults and three children want to book for the 2 day ticket for today's date of 19.01.08.

> **RECEIPT**
>
> 2 x adults, off-peak, 2 day ticket, gate ticket
> 3 x child, off-peak, 2 day ticket, gate ticket
>
> Dated 19.01.08

Is the receipt correct?

Question 33

One adult and three children arrive at the theme park 5 minutes before on-peak hours finish. They get to the ticket booth and ask for 1 day tickets. You look at the date which is the 15.05.10.

RECEIPT

1 x adult, on-peak, 1 day ticket, gate ticket
3 x child, on-peak, 1 day ticket, gate ticket

Dated 15.05.10

Does the receipt contain the correct information?

Question 34

Two adults and one child arrive at the theme park having already booked and paid for their tickets online. They arrive on the date of 04.06.12, during peak hours. They have purchased tickets for the mini fast track.

RECEIPT

2 x adult, on-peak, mini fast, gate ticket
1 x child, on-peak, mini fast, gate ticket

Dated 03.06.12

Is the receipt correct?

Question 35

Three families have come together for a child's birthday party. Each family has two adults and two children. They arrive on today's date of 31.01.14, during off-peak hours. They all just want standard one day tickets. However, they ask you if they can pay for each family separately, so you process their bookings individually. You hand back three receipts; one for each family.

RECEIPT 1

2 x adults, off-peak, 1 day gate ticket
2 x child, off-peak, 1 day gate ticket

Dated 31.01.14

RECEIPT 2

2 x adults, off-peak, 1 day gate ticket
2 x child, off-peak, 1 day gate ticket

Dated 31.01.14

RECEIPT 3

2 x adults, on-peak, 1 day gate ticket
2 x child, on-peak, 1 day gate ticket

Dated 31.01.14

Are all of the receipts correct?

Question 36

Two adults arrive at the park and want to purchase the 2 day tickets. They arrive during peak hours on the date 05.07.13.

> **RECEIPT**
>
> 2 x adults, on-peak, 1 day gate ticket
>
> Dated 05.07.13

Does the receipt contain the correct information?

Question 37

Two children, two adults and two seniors arrive at the park with already booking their tickets. You check their confirmation letter which tells you that they booked all tickets for the hydro fast track on the date 17.04.13. They booked these tickets during off-peak hours which they have arrived in time for.

> **RECEIPT**
>
> 2 x adults, off-peak, hydro fast, advance book
> 2 x child, off-peak, hydro fast, advance book
> 2 x seniors, off-peak, hydro fast, advance book
>
> Dated 17.04.13

Is the receipt correct?

Question 38

A group of fourteen adults arrive at the theme park for a hen party. They have booked in advance for today's date of 24.05.14. They have arrived during off-peak hours, which is what they booked in advance.

RECEIPT

14 x adults, off-peak, group ticket, advance book

Dated 24.05.14

Is the receipt accurate?

Question 39

It is the 02.03.13, and you have arrived half an hour early before off-peak hours begin. The theme park is just opening and you receive your first set of customers. Two adults and one child would like to book for the extreme fast track option. You ask them for the required amount of money, and hand them back a receipt.

RECEIPT

2 x adults, off-peak, extreme fast, gate ticket
1 x child, off-peak, extreme fast, gate ticket

Dated 02.03.13

Is the receipt accurate?

Question 40

A group of nine friends, who are classed as adults, want to book for the ultimate fast track. They have not made any bookings in advance, and have arrived during peak time. They ask if they can pay for three of them, the other three, and then the other three. So you need to make the booking three times, and process three receipts. The date is 05.10.10.

RECEIPT 1

3 x adults, on-peak, ultimate fast, gate ticket

Dated 05.10.10

RECEIPT 2

3 x adults, on-peak, ultimate fast, gate ticket

Dated 05.10.10

RECEIPT 3

9 x adults, on-peak, ultimate fast, gate ticket

Dated 05.10.10

Which receipt contains incorrect information?

Question 41

Four adults arrive on the 06.07.10. They wish to purchase tickets for fast track. However two of them want to purchase fast track tickets for hydro, and the other two want to purchase fast track options for ultimate. They arrive during peak hours.

RECEIPT

2 x adult, on-peak, ultimate fast, gate ticket
2 x adult, on-peak, hydro fast, gate ticket

Dated 06.07.10

Is the receipt correct?

Question 42

A group of 15 adults arrive at the park and want to purchase fast track tickets. The date is 19.03.13, and is during off-peak hours. Three of the people want to purchase hydro fast track tickets, five of them want to purchase the extreme fast track tickets and the remaining people want the ultimate fast track.

RECEIPT

3 x adults, off-peak, hydro fast, gate ticket
5 x adults, off-peak, extreme fast, gate ticket
6 x adults, off-peak, ultimate fast, gate ticket

Dated 19.03.13

Is the receipt correct?

Question 43

Two adults and four children arrive at the theme park. They arrive 10 minutes before opening, which means that they will only be charged for off-peak hours. They want to purchase the 2 day tickets, commencing from today's date of 16.05.13.

RECEIPT

2 x adults, off-peak, 2 day ticket, gate ticket
4 x child, off-peak, 2 day ticket, gate ticket

Dated 16.05.13

Is the receipt correct?

Question 44

A group of eight adults and six children arrive at the theme park having already booked their day tickets online. They arrive at the park on the scheduled date that is written in the confirmation letter, the 08.08.12. They have arrived during the time they booked for which was for off-peak hours. They paid using the best deal.

RECEIPT

8 x adults, off-peak, group ticket, advance book
6 x child, off-peak, group ticket, advance book

Dated 08.08.12

Is the information on the receipt accurate?

Question 45

Five children arrive at the ticket booth and ask to purchase five tickets for the hydro fast track. The date is 11.03.13, and you take note of the fact that it is past off-peak hours.

> **RECEIPT**
>
> 5 x child, on-peak, hydro fast, gate ticket
>
>   Dated 10.02.13

Does the receipt match the description of what the customers asked for?

Question 46

Five adults and three children book in advance for the 2 day ticket during on-peak hours. They arrive at the theme park and hand you their confirmation details. You notice that the tickets are valid for the 18.07.14. You also notice that they have arrived during on-peak hours.

> **RECEIPT**
>
> 5 x adults, on-peak, 2 day ticket, advance book
> 3 x child, on-peak, 2 day ticket, advance book
>
>   Dated 08.07.14

Is the receipt correct?

Question 47

Four adults arrive at the theme park and are deciding which tickets to purchase. They all opt to buy the ultimate fast track tickets. You tell them that they have arrived just after off-peak hours, so the price of the tickets will be slightly more. They wish to pay for their tickets separately, so you need to issue four individual receipts. The date is 07.08.13.

RECEIPT 1

1 x adult, on-peak, ultimate fast, gate ticket

Dated 07.08.13

RECEIPT 2

1 x adult, on-peak, ultimate fast, gate ticket

Dated 07.08.13

RECEIPT 3

1 x adult, on-peak, ultimate fast, gate ticket

Dated 07.08.13

RECEIPT 4

1 x adult, off-peak, ultimate fast, gate ticket

Dated 07.08.13

Are all of the receipts correct?

Question 48

Three adults wish to book for the ultimate fast track ticket during on-peak hours for the date 21.10.13. You process their entrance and hand them their receipt.

RECEIPT

3 x adults, on-peak, ultimate fast, gate ticket

Dated 21.10.13

Is the receipt correct?

Question 49

A family of two adults, two seniors and four children arrive at the theme park. They made a booking online and give you the confirmation details. They arrive at the park on the 11.05.08 during on-peak hours. They have all purchased hydro fast track tickets.

RECEIPT

2 x adults, on-peak, hydro fast, advance book
4 x child, on-peak, hydro fast, advance book
2 x seniors, on-peak, hydro fast, advance book

Dated 11.05.08

Is the receipt correct?

Question 50

Six adults arrive at the theme park and want to purchase fast track tickets. Two of them purchase the extreme fast track tickets, whereas the others purchase the ultimate fast track tickets. They have arrived just in time for off-peak hours. The date is 30.06.14.

> **RECEIPT**
>
> 2 x adults, off-peak, extreme fast, gate ticket
> 4 x adults, off-peak, extreme fast, gate ticket
>
> Dated 30.06.14

Is the receipt accurate?

Question 51

A group of ten people, six children and four adults arrive with a pre-booked group ticket. They have purchased tickets for on-peak hours for the date of 08.09.10.

> **RECEIPT**
>
> 4 x adults, off-peak, group ticket, gate ticket
> 6 x child, off-peak, group ticket, gate ticket
>
> Dated 08.09.10

Is the receipt correct?

Question 52

An adult and her child arrive at the theme park and wish to book tickets for the mini fast track. They have arrived on the 09.07.13, during off-peak hours.

> **RECEIPT**
>
> 1 x adult, off-peak, mini fast, gate ticket
> 1 x child, off-peak, mini fast, gate ticket
>
> Dated 09.07.13

Is the receipt accurate?

Question 53

Two adults and two children wish to purchase their tickets during on-peak hours. They have arrived on the 06.06.13, and wish to purchase the 2 day tickets.

> **RECEIPT**
>
> 2 x adults, on-peak, 1 day gate ticket
> 2 x child, on-peak, 1 day gate ticket
>
> Dated 06.06.13

Is the receipt correct?

Question 54

A group of twelve students, who are classed as adults arrive on the 11.06.13. They arrive during off-peak hours. They wish to purchase their tickets as a group.

> **RECEIPT**
>
> 12 x adults, off-peak, group ticket, gate ticket
>
>   Dated 11.06.13

Is the receipt correct?

Question 55

Two adults and two children visit the theme park. They have not made any bookings and wish to purchase the mini fast track tickets. They have just missed the off-peak hours. The date is 29.07.14.

> **RECEIPT**
>
> 2 x adults, off-peak, mini fast, gate ticket
> 2 x child, off-peak, mini fast, gate ticket
>
>   Dated 29.07.14

Does the receipt contain the correct information?

Question 56

One adult arrives at the park without no bookings. He wants to purchase a 2 day ticket for off-peak hours. The date is 17.08.12.

RECEIPT

1 x adult, off-peak, 2 day ticket, gate ticket

Dated 17.08.12

Is the receipt correct?

Question 57

Three adults and two seniors arrive at the park on the 13.04.11. They want to purchase 1 day ticket for off-peak hours.

RECEIPT

3 x adults, off-peak, 1 day ticket, gate ticket
2 x seniors, off-peak, 1 day ticket, gate ticket

Dated 13.04.11

Is the receipt correct?

Question 58

Four children and three adults arrive at the theme park for opening hours. Because they are there for opening, they receive off peak hour prices. The children have fast track tickets for hydro, and the three adults have tickets for extreme fast track. The date is 19.07.14.

RECEIPT

3 x adults, off-peak, extreme fast, gate ticket
4 x child, off-peak, hydro fast, gate ticket

Dated 19.07.14

Is the receipt correct?

Question 59

One adult arrives with their only child and has booked for mini fast track tickets in advance. They arrive on the 02.05.10, during off-peak hours.

RECEIPT

1 x adult, off-peak, mini fast, advance book
1 x child, off-peak, mini fast, advance book

Dated 02.05.10

Is the information on the receipt correct?

Question 60

A group of four friends have arrived at the theme park, 20 minutes before on-peak hours. They all wish to purchase the ultimate fast track ticket. However, they ask if they can pay separately, so you put the transaction through individually. The date is 08.11.14.

RECEIPT 1

1 x adult, off-peak, ultimate fast, gate ticket

Dated 08.11.14

RECEIPT 2

1 x adult, off-peak, ultimate fast, gate ticket

Dated 08.11.14

RECEIPT 3

1 x adult, off-peak, ultimate fast, gate ticket

Dated 08.11.14

RECEIPT 4

1 x adult, off-peak, ultimate fast, gate ticket

Dated 08.11.14

Are all of the receipts correct?

ANSWERS TO DOCUMENT AUDIT TEST

Q1. Yes

Q2. No (the receipt should say that they purchased the 2 day tickets).

Q3. No (the receipt should say an adult).

Q4. Yes

Q5. Yes

Q6. No (there are 3 children; they purchased 1 day tickets).

Q7. Yes

Q8. No (incorrect date on receipt).

Q9. No (they arrived during on-peak hours).

Q10. No (there are 2 children; they booked in advance; incorrect date).

Q11. No (there are 3 adults, not children; purchased ultimate fast track; incorrect date).

Q12. No (they booked for off-peak; incorrect date).

Q13. No (incorrect date).

Q14. Yes

Q15. No (date incorrect).

Q16. No (they booked for hydro fast track).

Q17. No (they booked in advance).

Q18. Yes

Q19. No (there are 3 adults and 5 children; incorrect date).

Q20. Yes

Q21. Yes

Q22. No (receipt 2 there should be 10 adults).

Q23. No (they arrive for off-peak hours).

Q24. Yes

Q25. Yes

Q26. No (they arrive during on-peak hours).

Q27. Yes

Q28. Yes

Q29. Yes

Q30. No (receipt 2 should be for the 2 day ticket).

Q31. No (they arrive during peak hours).

Q32. No (they arrive during peak hours).

Q33. Yes

Q34. No (booked in advance; incorrect date).

Q35. No (receipt 3 should be for off-peak hours).

Q36. No (they purchased the 2 day tickets).

Q37. Yes

Q38. Yes

Q39. Yes

Q40. Receipt 3 (should only be for 3 people, not 9).

Q41. Yes

Q42. No (there should be 7 adults charged for the ultimate fast track).

Q43. Yes

Q44. Yes

Q45. No (incorrect date, should be for off-peak hours).

Q46. No (incorrect date).

Q47. No (receipt 4 should be for on-peak hours).

Q48. Yes

Q49. Yes

Q50. Yes

Q51. No (they booked in advance, booked for on-peak hours).

Q52. Yes

Q53. No (they purchased the 2 day ticket).

Q54. Yes

Q55. No (they booked during on-peak hours).

Q56. Yes

Q57. Yes

Q58. Yes

Q59. Yes

Q60. Yes

THE ROLE-PLAY EXERCISES

There is no substitute for observing a candidate in a real-time customer interaction and the role-plays are specifically designed for the Train Operating Company to determine whether or not a candidate has the potential to become a competent Conductor.

There are 6 different versions of role play scenario that the assessor can choose from. Each version is different, using slightly different props, but the competencies being assessed are the same, allowing easy rating for the assessor. The actual role play is conducted one-to-one.

During the role play you will have to deal with a number of real-life situations that a Train Conductor would be expected to deal with during their working day. The type of situation that you will be confronted with varies greatly. However, examples of the types of exercises that have been used in the past include the following:

- A passenger who is becoming verbally abusive and aggressive;
- A passenger who does not have a valid ticket for their journey;
- A passenger who becomes ill during the journey;
- A passenger who is under the influence of alcohol;
- A passenger who is becoming angry because the train is delayed;
- A passenger who refuses to move from First Class travel, despite not having a valid ticket to travel in this section of the train.

The situation that you will have to deal with is irrelevant. It is how you interact with the role play actor and what you

say that is important. You must be able to demonstrate the competencies being assessed during each role-play scenario. Examples of how you would achieve this include:

- Dealing with the role play actor in a sensitive and supportive manner;

- Challenging any language or behaviour which was inappropriate;

- Having respect for people's views and feelings;

- Seeing issues from others' points of view;

- Demonstrating an excellent level of customer-service;

- Remaining calm and in control at all times;

- Asking relevant questions to clarify the situation;

- Listening to passengers' needs and interests;

- Respecting confidentiality where appropriate;

- Presenting an appropriate image of the Train Operating Company;

- Trying to sort out passengers' problems as soon as possible;

- Making reference to any supporting documentation, policies or procedures;

- Confirming that the passenger is happy with your offered solution.

- Keeping passengers' updated on any progress that you make and also update them in regards to any delays.

Having personally been through this type of role play assessment I found that by learning the role of a Train Conductor it made my life a lot easier.

Here is a step-by-step process for dealing with the role play scenario:

STEP 1 – Introduce yourself to the role actor
and ask him/her how you can help them.
(Remember to be polite and respectful and treat the role play actor in a sensitive and supportive manner. You are being assessed on the competencies of respect for passengers and also customer-service during every role play scenario)

STEP 2 – Listen to them carefully and ask
relevant questions to establish the facts.
(How, When, Where, Why, Who)

STEP 3 – Clarify the information received to check you have understood exactly what has happened.

STEP 4 – Provide a suitable solution to the problem or situation and tell the role play actor what you intend to do.

STEP 5 – Check to confirm that the role play actor is happy with your solution.
Provide a final summary of what you intend to do and ask them if there is anything else you can help them with.

TOP TIPS FOR PREPARING FOR THE ROLE-PLAY EXERCISES

- Learn the competencies that are being assessed and be able to 'act' out each one. You should also have a thorough understanding of the role of a Train Conductor.

- A good way to practise for these exercises is to get a friend or family relative to 'role-play' the sample role play scenarios I mentioned at the beginning of this section.

- When practising the exercises, try to pick someone you know who will make it difficult for you. Also, try to resolve each issue in a calm but effective manner, in line with the core competencies.

- Learn the pre-assessment material before you go to the assessment (if provided). This will make your life much easier.

- Remain calm during every role-play. Even if the actor becomes confrontational, it is essential that you remain calm.

- If at any time during the role play activity phase the role play actor uses language that is either inappropriate (including swearing), discriminatory or uses any form of harassment then you must challenge it immediately. When challenging this kind of behaviour you must do so in an assertive manner without becoming aggressive. Always be polite and respectful at all times.

- Use effective listening skills during the role-play exercises and ask questions in order to gather the facts.

- Once you have gathered the facts of the case or situation then solve the problem.

CONCENTRATION TESTS

During the Train Conductor selection process/assessment centre you may have to undertake a form of concentration test. These concentration tests will be used to determine how well you can concentrate for long periods of time.

Within this section I have created a number of tests that will help you prepare specifically for concentration tests. This is probably the hardest part of the testing process. It is the one test that most people fail and this is mainly due to a lack of preparation. Many candidates turn up to take the test without any prior knowledge of how it works and what is expected of them.

The test is designed to assess your ability to concentrate whilst performing tasks at a fast speed, such as checking tickets whilst carrying out your duties as a Train Conductor. The test will be carried out either with a pen and paper, or a computer and a computer screen. Whichever test you undertake, you will be presented with five pages or screens that each contains 25 columns. Each of the columns contains boxes with patterns of dots which are either in groups of 2, 3, 4, 5 or 6. Your task is to work quickly and accurately through each column, from left to right, identifying boxes of 4 dots only.

You are allowed two minutes only per sheet and, once the two minutes are up, you are told to move onto the next page regardless of whether you have completed it or not. The test requires ten minutes of solid concentration.

Take a look at the following row of dots:

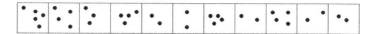

You will notice that the 2nd, 4th, 7th and 9th boxes each contain 4 dots. If you were taking the paper and pencil based version of the test, you would mark the boxes that contain 4 dots as follows:

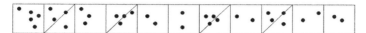

You will notice that I have placed a single diagonal line through each of the boxes that contains 4 dots.

If you are required to undertake the computer based version of the test then you will be required to use the keys on the keyboard as follows:

 You will use this key to move from left to right across the screen.

 You will use this key to mark each box that contains 4 dots.

 You will use this key to move back in order to correct any mistakes.

On the following pages I have provided you with ten sample concentration tests. During the first set of five concentration tests you are required to locate specific letters and/or numbers that are contained within rows and columns. Full instructions are provided at the start of each test.

During the second set of five concentration tests, you will be required to search for groups of 4 dots in rows and columns of boxes. Once again, full instructions are provided.

SAMPLE CONCENTRATION TEST 1

Cross out the letter 'R' (upper case) in each row. Write down the total number that you cross out in each row in the box provided at the end of each row. You have 60 seconds to complete the test.

1.	Q	r	R	g	y	U	h	J	R	j	R	k	L	B	n
2.	R	R	R	v	B	n	M	U	u	d	f	O	p	T	R
3.	C	x	X	F	R	G	t	p	A	R	f	V	R	y	U
4.	Q	R	R	t	G	N	H	J	r	r	F	P	F	R	r
5.	Q	a	Z	x	R	t	I	o	M	B	R	D	x	A	S
6.	R	s	a	A	e	E	R	C	Y	U	r	j	P	o	R
7.	T	R	r	P	F	r	S	N	b	V	c	F	F	R	R
8.	G	v	R	r	R	y	R	P	R	r	D	e	E	R	F
9.	T	R	K	P	o	u	b	g	t	m	R	r	X	r	R
10.	C	B	n	h	j	Y	I	p	R	R	R	r	R	C	d
11.	R	R	r	Y	u	B	v	M	n	h	K	j	R	E	R
12.	A	W	r	E	R	f	p	U	I	H	R	y	U	B	R
13.	R	r	Q	q	B	G	R	t	Q	w	E	F	T	y	R
14.	T	R	A	I	N	D	P	I	V	E	R	D	T	y	S
15.	d	x	z	Z	R	n	K	i	i	R	r	R	O	p	o
16.	Q	R	r	E	D	D	e	w	K	i	I	O	P	R	R
17	H	O	w	B	e	E	R	r	R	R	V	R	H	j	R
18.	K	j	u	U	Y	i	Y	r	R	R	D	X	z	q	Q
19.	P	y	g	h	j	I	r	t	r	e	R	e	R	q	Z
20.	B	h	B	h	r	r	R	r	N	B	H	y	Y	R	F

SAMPLE CONCENTRATION TEST 2

Cross out the letter 'o' (lower case). Write down the total number that you cross out in each row in the box provided at the end of each row. You have 60 seconds to complete the test.

1.	o	O	t	Q	w	q	O	o	A	B	u	U	o	o	O	
2.	O	o	g	Y	t	B	c	C	c	O	o	o	o	D	w	
3.	B	o	O	g	a	s	S	q	Q	t	Q	q	O	o	G	
4.	I	L	N	h	U	u	O	o	H	y	t	R	o	O	o	
5.	G	V	v	R	t	Y	o	o	P	i	O	O	o	O	R	
6.	G	t	y	U	J	P	p	O	o	D	d	O	o	S	Q	
7.	O	o	O	o	o	o	Y	t	Y	q	Q	q	o	c	c	
8.	I	u	V	c	c	F	r	d	w	H	y	h	u	o	o	
9.	Y	o	o	U	o	O	O	y	D	e	q	A	q	O	o	
10.	R	r	t	o	u	y	G	b	t	r	e	o	o	o	P	
11.	o	O	c	o	d	d	D	O	c	c	O	o	o	d	R	
12.	B	v	c	f	R	o	y	f	D	r	d	r	a	A	a	
13.	F	t	t	t	d	r	e	o	o	p	u	o	Q	t	r	
14.	F	g	r	t	y	N	H	N	h	o	p	O	o	I	y	
15.	T	r	e	d	w	o	u	i	y	F	c	r	D	e	W	
16.	o	o	O	o	p	O	u	i	S	t	d	r	s	S	O	
17.	I	o	O	A	a	a	c	C	c	g	o	o	o	R	t	
18.	G	g	g	g	o	t	f	d	r	t	u	u	o	o	j	
19.	Q	c	v	b	g	t	y	u	O	o	O	o	G	y	c	
20.	K	l	o	i	u	y	t	r	e	o	u	y	o	j	h	

SAMPLE CONCENTRATION TEST 3

Cross out the letters 'w' (lower case) and 'V' (upper case). Search for both of these letters at the same time. Write down the total combined number that you cross out in each row in the box provided at the end of each row. You have 60 seconds to complete the test.

1.	v	W	w	V	e	w	h	j	U	i	X	x	W	w	v	
2.	V	u	U	w	G	t	y	u	W	w	V	v	W	o	o	
3.	W	W	V	V	v	v	w	w	y	u	i	p	v	W	W	
4.	V	g	h	j	K	O	p	t	Y	V	v	W	W	w	V	
5.	Y	U	u	u	v	v	W	M	m	w	e	V	v	N	n	
6.	q	q	Q	G	g	H	Y	u	i	R	T	y	V	w	v	
7.	V	y	u	Y	u	o	p	N	h	j	W	w	V	V	v	
8.	t	y	m	k	m	N	b	C	x	W	w	V	v	b	v	
9.	O	o	V	v	f	g	h	j	k	n	h	N	h	V	X	
10.	T	V	v	X	c	d	W	w	W	v	V	v	f	r	p	
11.	V	V	v	w	W	w	v	V	v	W	w	g	y	Y	v	
12.	R	t	y	u	i	B	g	v	f	r	D	r	Q	w	W	
13.	R	t	y	V	c	V	c	v	f	r	W	w	W	w	V	
14.	G	y	u	i	O	p	R	t	y	E	w	V	V	v	W	
15.	Y	Y	y	Y	X	v	W	W	w	w	r	t	y	u	v	
16.	W	w	w	v	t	u	i	n	h	v	V	w	W	w	f	
17.	r	t	y	y	u	i	V	b	n	h	g	w	w	W	w	
18.	i	o	q	w	S	S	X	W	V	Z	z	V	v	W	y	
19.	P	o	Y	u	i	V	v	X	w	W	w	R	t	R	y	
20.	y	u	V	x	s	t	Y	u	y	W	w	C	d	V	w	

SAMPLE CONCENTRATION TEST 4

Cross out the number 8 and the letter 'b' (lower case). Search for both letter and number at the same time. Write down the total combined number that you cross out in each row in the box provided at the end of each row. You have 60 seconds to complete the test.

1.	8	B	8	V	v	W	q	P	p	r	g	B	b	8	u	
2.	B	b	R	r	r	y	U	i	8	8	B	B	b	g	G	
3.	j	u	p	P	b	v	f	r	B	b	w	3	6	7	R	
4.	8	3	2	h	y	U	x	W	w	v	x	v	b	B	8	
5.	f	G	g	B	p	h	b	b	b	B	B	8	8	5	3	
6.	y	u	U	7	6	5	8	e	r	d	r	w	8	B	b	
7.	o	O	o	P	7	8	5	b	3	8	3	R	r	S	l	
8.	B	b	3	8	B	B	b	h	h	V	c	b	B	7	1	
9.	1	3	c	V	f	l	u	y	t	r	B	b	8	8	8	
10.	y	B	b	8	4	3	3	3	X	x	x	f	F	r	t	
11.	Q	q	H	b	B	b	8	B	6	3	3	2	u	B	b	
12.	G	G	g	B	b	8	3	8	3	D	d	D	l	P	p	
13.	G	b	b	8	8	6	5	4	0	L	o	P	p	P	B	
14	3	B	b	8	3	B	B	b	3	E	e	3	8	4	P	
15.	t	Y	y	D	e	e	D	f	g	W	8	8	P	P	B	
16.	C	C	b	n	B	8	B	8	B	b	8	3	9	3	9	
17.	6	6	b	B	8	8	d	k	l	p	o	U	S	y	Y	
18.	P	p	8	F	d	D	c	C	8	B	b	8	f	F	f	
19.	8	8	C	f	z	s	W	w	R	r	T	8	3	B	b	
20.	H	y	y	b	B	8	8	8	H	H	h	D	r	e	W	

SAMPLE CONCENTRATION TEST 5

Cross out the letter 'e' (lower case) and the number '3'. Search for both letter and number at the same time. Write down the number crossed out in the box provided at the end of each row. You have 60 seconds to complete the test.

1.	E	6	e	8	8	e	3	p	b	d	e	E	3	8	T	
2.	e	8	3	6	7	y	u	I	V	f	E	e	b	B	E	
3.	W	w	q	D	d	c	x	z	O	p	e	R	6	8	3	
4.	y	u	I	o	p	P	t	T	Y	e	E	3	8	6	F	
5.	g	B	4	3	2	7	8	3	e	E	3	4	E	e	3	
6.	e	3	3	e	E	d	W	q	h	j	K	8	7	N	9	
7.	3	e	E	8	B	8	3	e	E	k	K	3	e	8	7	
8.	f	C	x	b	g	t	T	r	6	8	3	4	X	d	e	
9.	3	3	3	b	8	b	e	3	E	3	8	3	4	0	1	
10.	e	E	j	H	g	b	3	E	e	3	w	b	V	v	E	
11.	8	3	B	v	C	f	v	e	8	4	3	3	3	e	v	
12.	6	7	8	v	c	D	f	3	7	8	6	E	e	e	V	
13.	e	3	e	3	E	8	E	3	e	E	3	2	8	G	g	
14.	7	y	h	n	g	f	d	e	E	4	E	e	3	D	d	
15	k	I	L	j	h	y	V	v	8	4	2	b	V	v	E	
16.	g	Y	y	i	9	8	7	0	3	O	o	v	V	v	e	
17.	8	2	B	b	v	e	W	e	r	5	5	R	r	e	V	
18.	3	e	E	e	3	4	b	V	v	e	W	w	q	A	a	
19.	5	e	3	V	f	r	6	5	4	e	e	E	e	3	E	
20.	e	E	e	R	3	4	2	1	3	E	e	h	G	f	d	

ANSWERS TO CONCENTRATION TESTS

Row #	TEST 1	TEST 2	TEST 3	TEST 4	TEST 5
1.	3	4	4	4	5
2.	4	4	4	4	3
3.	3	2	4	2	2
4.	3	3	4	3	2
5.	2	3	2	5	6
6.	3	2	2	3	4
7.	3	5	4	3	6
8.	5	2	2	4	2
9.	3	4	2	4	7
10.	4	4	3	2	4
11.	4	4	6	4	6
12.	3	1	1	3	3
13.	3	3	5	4	7
14.	2	2	3	4	3
15	3	1	2	2	0
16.	3	3	5	5	2
17.	5	4	4	3	3
18.	2	3	3	4	5
19.	2	2	3	4	6
20.	2	3	4	4	5

Check through your answers carefully and go back to check over the ones you got wrong.

Now move on to the next section of concentration tests.

SAMPLE DOTS CONCENTRATION TEST 1

Place a diagonal line across each box that contains 4 dots only. You have 30 seconds to complete the test.

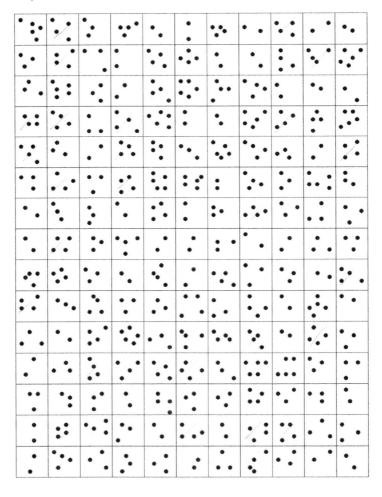

SAMPLE DOTS CONCENTRATION TEST 2

Place a diagonal line across each box that contains 4 dots only. You have 30 seconds to complete the test.

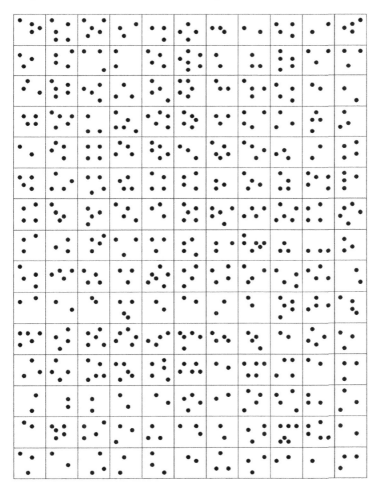

SAMPLE DOTS CONCENTRATION TEST 3

Place a diagonal line across each box that contains 4 dots only. You have 30 seconds to complete the test.

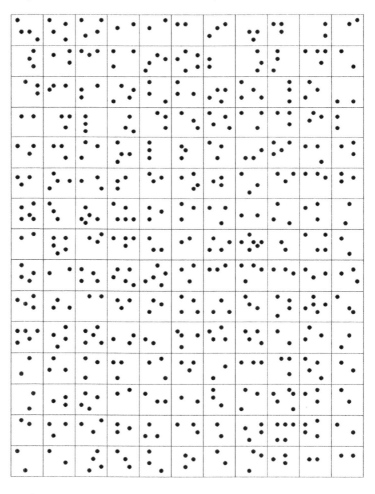

SAMPLE DOTS CONCENTRATION TEST 4

Place a diagonal line across each box that contains 4 dots only. You have 30 seconds to complete the test.

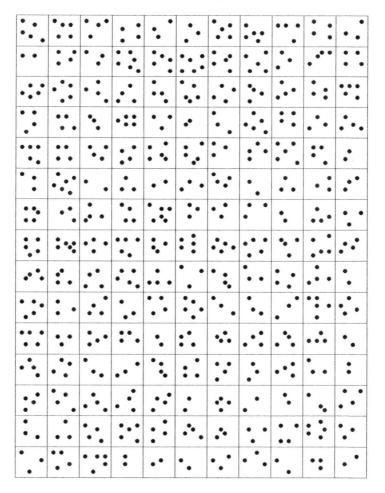

SAMPLE DOTS CONCENTRATION TEST 5

Place a diagonal line across each box that contains 4 dots only. You have 30 seconds to complete the test.

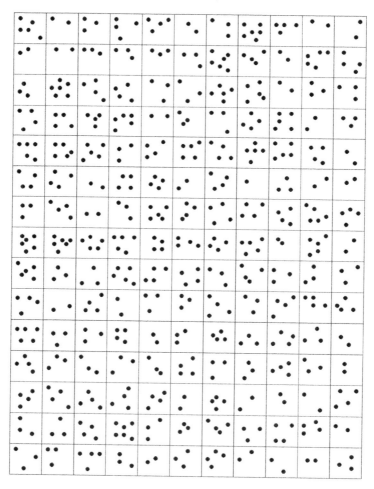

ANSWERS TO DOTS CONCENTRATION TESTS 1 TO 5

DOTS CONCENTRATION TEST 1
56 boxes containing groups of 4 dots

DOTS CONCENTRATION TEST 2
58 boxes containing groups of 4 dots

DOTS CONCENTRATION TEST 3
31 boxes containing groups of 4 dots

DOTS CONCENTRATION TEST 4
66 boxes containing groups of 4 dots

DOTS CONCENTRATION TEST 5
56 boxes containing groups of 4 dots

CHAPTER SIX

THE INTERVIEW

During this section of the guide I will provide you with some useful tips on how to prepare for the Train Conductor interviews. The information provided will be useful for both the initial selection interview and also the structured interview.

The Train Conductor interview does not have to be a daunting process, providing that you prepare effectively. Yes, any interview can be a nerve-wracking experience, but if you prepare in the right areas this will give the confidence you need to pass with flying colours. Within this section of the guide I have provided you with a number of sample questions that you may get asked during your interview. The structured interview may be carried out on the same day as the assessment centre, so make sure you have prepared for it well in advance.

HOW TO PREPARE EFFECTIVELY

During your preparation for the interview I would recommend that you concentrate on the following three key areas:

- Interview technique;

- Research;

- Responding to the interview questions.

Each of the above areas are equally important. I will now go into each one of them in detail:

INTERVIEW TECHNIQUE

Interview technique covers a number of different areas. The majority of candidates will pay it little, if any attention at all. Interview technique basically involves the following key areas:

- **Creating the right impression.** When you walk into the interview room you should stand up tall, smile and be polite and courteous to the panel. Do not sit down in the interview chair until invited to do so.

- **Being presentable.** During my time as an interviewer for a number of different jobs I have been amazed at the number of people who turn up inappropriately dressed. I have seen people turn up for interviews in jeans, t shirts and trainers! I strongly advise that you take the time to look smart and presentable. Remember you are applying to join an organisation that requires you to wear a uniform. If you dress smart and formal for the interview then you are far more likely to wear your uniform with pride.

- **Sitting in the chair.** The interview could last for up to an hour, depending on the length of your responses to the questions. This is a long time to concentrate for. Whilst in the interview chair sit up right at all times and never slouch.

- **Motivation.** Throughout the duration of the interview demonstrate a high level of motivation and enthusiasm. You do not want to come across as desperate, but conversely you must come across as highly motivated and determined to be successful. Always smile and be respectful of the interview panel.

- **Communication.** When communicating with the interview panel look them in the eye. This shows a level of confidence. You should also communicate in a clear and concise manner where possible. Remember that one of the key requirements for the role of a Train Conductor is that of effective communication.

- **Asking questions.** At the end of the interview you will be given the opportunity to ask questions. This is where some candidates let themselves down with silly or inappropriate questions that relate to leave or sick pay. It is quite acceptable to ask a couple of questions, however, keep them simple and relevant. Examples of good questions to ask are:

Q. If I am successful, how long would it be before I start my training as a Train Conductor?

Q. I have been looking into your company and I have been impressed with the 'meet the manager's' scheme that you operate for your customers. Has this been successful?

Q. Whilst I wait to hear whether or not I am successful,

is there any additional literature or information I could study and read about the train operating company to further my knowledge?

- **A final parting statement.** Once the interview has finished and you have asked your questions, you may wish to finish off with a final statement. Your final statement should say something about your desire and passion for becoming a Train Conductor. The following is a good example of a final statement:

"I would like to say thank you for giving me the opportunity to be interviewed for the post today. Over the last few months I have been working hard to learn about the role and also about your company. If I am successful then I promise you that I will be a loyal and professional employee of your team. Thank you."

RESEARCH

As you can imagine, in the build-up to the interview you will need to carry out plenty of research. Research, that is, in relation to the role of a Train Conductor and also the Train Operating Company that you are applying to join. Here is a list of the more important areas I recommend that you study:

- The job description and person specification for the job that you are applying for.

- Your application form and the responses that you provided to all of the questions.

- The website of the Train Operating Company you are applying to join. What is their customer service charter? Do they have a mission statement? What services do they provide? What is their geographical area? How

many people work for them? Who is the person in charge? What stations do they operate out of? What trains do they operate? Do they operate any schemes in order to improve customer service? What are the future plans of the TOC?

- Try to visit a train station that the TOC operates out of. Speak to some of the staff at the station and ask them questions about the role they perform. Try to find out as much as possible about the TOC you are applying for. If you get the opportunity, speak to a qualified Train Conductor who works for the TOC. You may also decide to telephone the TOCs Human Resources department and ask if you can go along to find out a little bit more about their organisation and what they expect from their employees.

RESPONDING TO THE INTERVIEW QUESTIONS

If I were preparing for the Train Conductor interview right now, I would take each area of the role individually and prepare a detailed response setting out where I meet the requirements of it.

Your response to each question that relates to the role must be 'specific' in nature. This means that you need to provide an example of where you have already demonstrated the skills that are required under the job description or person specification in a previous role or situation. Do not fall into the trap of providing a 'generic' response that details what you 'would do' if the situation arose. Try to structure your responses in a logical and concise manner. The way to achieve this is to use the 'STAR' method of interview question response construction:

Situation

Start off your response to the interview question by explaining what the 'situation' was and who was involved.

Task

Once you have detailed the situation, explain what the 'task' was, or what needed to be done.

Action

Now explain what 'action' you took, and what action others took. Also explain why you took this particular course of action.

Result

Now explain what the outcome or result was following your actions and those of others. Try to demonstrate in your response that the result was positive because of the action you took.

Finally, explain to the panel what you would do differently if the same situation arose again. It is good to be reflective at the end of your responses. This demonstrates a level of maturity and it will also show the panel that you are willing to learn from every experience.

THE DIFFERENT TYPES OF INTERVIEW QUESTIONS

Basically there are two different types of interview questions that you could be asked. I will try to explain each of them and what they mean:

1. Generic questions about you and your knowledge of the TOC and the Train Conductors role

Generic questions can be in any format. There is no particular

structure to this type of question but they are generally far easier to respond to. Examples of generic questions would include:

- Why do you want to become a Train Conductor?

- What has attracted you to this TOC in particular?

- What have you learnt about the role?

- Why should we choose you against the other applicants?

2. Role related questions

This type of question is more common during the structured interview and includes questions that are based around the job description/person specification. Examples of role related questions include:

- Being able to work under pressure.

- Following rules or guidelines.

- Providing a high level of customer care and service.

- Working as part of a team to achieve a task.

- Communicating a message to a group of people.

- Working with people from different backgrounds.

- Dealing with difficult and aggressive people.

- Being flexible in a work-related situation.

On the following pages I have provided you with a number of sample interview questions and responses to assist you in your preparation. Please remember that the responses provided are not to be copied under any circumstances. Use them as a basis for your preparation taking examples from your own individual experiences and knowledge.

SAMPLE INTERVIEW QUESTIONS AND RESPONSES

QUESTION 1 – WHY DO YOU WANT TO BECOME A TRAIN CONDUCTOR?

This question is inevitable, so it is important that you ensure you have a suitable answer prepared. Many people will respond with a standard answer such as "It's something that I've always wanted do since I was young". Whilst this is OK you need to back it up with genuine reasons that relate to the TOC you are applying for and other important reasons such as working in a customer-focused environment and a desire to learn new skills.

This type of question may be posed in a number of different formats such as the following:

Q. Why do you want to become a Train Conductor with our Company?

Q. What has attracted you to the role of a Train Conductor?

Now take a look at the following sample response which will help you to prepare for this type of question. Once you have read it, use the template on the next page to create your own response based upon your own experiences and knowledge.

SAMPLE RESPONSE – Why do you want to become a Train Conductor?

"I have wanted to become a Train Conductor for many years now and have been preparing for the role for a long time. I have been very careful about which TOC to apply for and I have been impressed with the way your company operates. It sets itself high standards in terms of customer service and the safety standards that are expected of its employees. Apart from the fact that being a Train Conductor is quite a varied and responsible job, I also very much enjoy new and different

challenges. I understand that as a Train Conductor there are a lot of new skills to learn, especially during the early years. The type of person I am means that I would work hard to ensure that I passed every exam first time. I also enjoy working in a customer-focused environment where a high level of service is essential. As a Train Conductor you are responsible for the customer's comfort and safety and I would enjoy the high level of responsibility that comes with the position."

TEMPLATE FOR QUESTION 1 –
WHY DO YOU WANT TO BECOME A TRAIN CONDUCTOR?

QUESTION 2 – WHY DO YOU WANT TO WORK FOR OUR COMPANY?

Once again this is a question that is likely to come up during your interview. In order to prepare for this question you need to carry out some research about the TOC you are applying for. The best place to get this information is via their website. See the Useful Contacts section for a list of current TOCs.

When responding to this type of question, try to focus on the positive aspects of the company's work. Do they run any customer-focused initiatives or have they won any awards for quality of work or service? It is always good to make reference to the positive aspects of their work, but do not mention any current or previous bad press. I have now provided a sample response to this question to help you prepare. I have used Southern Rail as an example when constructing the response. Once you have read it, take the time to construct your own answer using the template provided.

SAMPLE RESPONSE – Why do you want to work for our company?

"I have been looking at a number of TOCs and I have been especially impressed with Southern Rail. The 'Meet the Managers' programme gives passengers the chance to meet Senior Managers and Directors and talk with them about the service. This demonstrates a high level of customer focus and care and I want to work for such a company as I believe I can bring the same high standards to the team.

I also understand that, over the next two years, Southern Rail aims to create a company that not only looks and feels different, but provides passengers with a better travelling experience. I believe that, whilst working with Southern Rail, I would have excellent career opportunities and therefore be very happy in my role as a Train Conductor."

TEMPLATE FOR QUESTION 2 – WHY DO YOU WANT TO WORK FOR OUR COMPANY?

QUESTION 3 – WHAT CAN YOU TELL US ABOUT THE ROLE OF A TRAIN CONDUCTOR?

You must be well-prepared for this question prior to your interview. If you don't know what the role involves, then you shouldn't be applying for the post. When responding to this question, make sure you make reference to the job/person specification for the role. The job specification is a 'blueprint' for the role that you will be required to perform whilst working as a Train Conductor. Therefore, it is essential that you know it. An example of a Train Conductors duties/person specification is detailed below:

TRAIN CONDUCTOR JOB DESCRIPTION AND PERSON SPECIFICATION

Train Conductors, also known as guards or train crew, make sure that rail passengers have paid their fare, and are safe and comfortable during their journey.

As a conductor, your day-to-day duties would include:

- Checking the carriages are clean before the start of a journey.

- Making sure equipment, doors and controls are working properly.

- Walking through carriages during the journey, checking tickets and travel documents.

- Answering passengers' questions about routes, arrival times and connections.

- Making announcements over the public address system.

- Making sure passengers get on and off the train safely.

- Dealing with unexpected delays or emergencies, for example a passenger falling ill.

You would also write reports, detailing any delays or incidents that occur during each journey.

Skills and knowledge

- Excellent customer service skills.

- A pleasant manner and smart appearance.

- A good understanding of rail regulations, safety procedures, fares and timetables.

- A clear speaking voice for making passenger announcements.

- The ability to accept responsibility and work without supervision.

- The ability to deal professionally with upset or angry passengers.

- Good maths skills for handling cash and payments.

- A willingness to work flexibly.

Now take a look at the sample response before constructing your own response using the template provided.

SAMPLE RESPONSE – What can you tell us about the role of a Train Conductor?

"I understand that the role involves a high level of responsibility, concentration and customer focus. To begin with, Train Conductors are responsible for checking the carriages are clean before the start of a journey, making sure equipment, doors and controls are working properly, walking through carriages during the journey, checking tickets and travel documents and also answering passengers' questions about

routes, arrival times and connections. In addition to this they must make announcements over the public address system, make sure passengers get on and off the train safely and dealing with unexpected delays or emergencies, for example a passenger falling ill. It is a highly responsible job that requires a level of flexibility, good concentration skills and an ability to deal with pressurised situations. It is also important that Train Conductors act as role models for the Train Operating Company as we want passengers to come back and use the service time and time again."

TEMPLATE FOR QUESTION 3 – WHAT CAN YOU TELL US ABOUT THE ROLE OF A TRAIN CONDUCTOR?

QUESTION 4 – WHAT SKILLS DO YOU POSSESS THAT YOU THINK WOULD BE AN ASSET TO OUR TEAM?

When responding to questions of this nature, try to match your skills with the skills that are required of a Train Conductor. On some TOC websites, you will be able to see the type of person they are looking to employ, usually in the recruitment section.

An example of this would be: 'We are looking for friendly, supportive people who share our professional, customer-focused approach. You must be a good team player with a flexible attitude and a willingness to learn.' Just by looking at the TOC's website, you should be able to obtain some clues as to the type of person they are seeking to employ. Try to think of the skills that are required to perform the role you are applying for and include them in your response.

The following is a sample response to the question. Once you have read it, take the time to construct your own response using the template provided.

SAMPLE RESPONSE – What skills do you possess that you think would be an asset to our team?

"I am a very conscientious person who takes the time to learn and develop new skills correctly. I have vast experience working in a customer-focused environment and fully understand that customer satisfaction is important. Without the customer there would be no company, so it is important that every member of the team works towards providing a high level of service.

I believe I have the skills, knowledge and experience to do this. I am a very good team player and can always be relied upon to carry out my role to the highest of standards. I am a flexible person and understand that there is a need to be available at

short notice to cover duties if required. In addition to these skills and attributes, I am a very good communicator. I have experience of having to communicate to customers in my previous role and believe that this would be an asset in the role of a Train Conductor. I am highly safety conscious and have a health and safety qualification to my name. Therefore, I can be relied upon to perform all procedures relevant to the codes of conduct and will not put myself or others in any danger whatsoever. Finally, I am very good at learning new skills which means that I will work hard to pass all of my exams if I am successful in becoming a trainee Train Conductor."

TEMPLATE FOR QUESTION 4 – WHAT SKILLS DO YOU POSSESS THAT YOU THINK WOULD BE AN ASSET TO OUR TEAM?

QUESTION 5 – CAN YOU TELL US ABOUT A SITUATION WHEN YOU HAVE HAD TO WORK UNDER PRESSURE?

The role of a Train Conductor will sometimes involve a requirement to work under pressure. Therefore, the recruitment staff will want to know that you have the ability to perform in such an environment. If you have experience of working under pressure then you are far more likely to succeed as a Train Conductor. When responding to a question of this nature, try to provide an actual example of where you have achieved a task whilst being under pressure. Questions of this nature are sometimes included in the application form, so try to use a different example for the interview.

I have provided you with a sample response to this question. Once you have read it, take the time to construct your own response based on your own individual experiences and knowledge using the template provided.

SAMPLE RESPONSE – Can you tell us about a situation when you have had to work under pressure?

"Yes, I can. In my current job as a car mechanic for a well-known company, I was presented with a difficult and pressurised situation. A member of the team had made a mistake and had fitted a number of wrong components to a car. The car in question was due to be picked up at 2pm and the customer had stated how important it was that his car was ready on time because he had an important meeting to attend.

We only had two hours in which to resolve the issue and I volunteered to be the one who would carry out the work on the car. The problem was that we had three other customers in the workshop waiting for their cars too, so I was the only person who could be spared at that particular time. I worked

solidly for the next two hours making sure that I meticulously carried out each task in line with our operating procedures. Even though I didn't finish the car until 2.10pm, I managed to achieve a very difficult task under pressurised conditions whilst keeping strictly to procedures and regulations."

TEMPLATE FOR QUESTION 5 – CAN YOU TELL US ABOUT A SITUATION WHEN YOU HAD TO WORK UNDER PRESSURE?

QUESTION 6 – CAN YOU TELL ME ABOUT A TIME WHEN YOU HAVE WORKED AS PART OF A TEAM TO ACHIEVE A GOAL?

Having the ability to work as part of a team is very important to the role of a Train Conductor. Train Operating Companies employ many people in different roles from Train Drivers to platform staff and from ticket office staff to cleaners. In fact it is not uncommon for thousands of people to work for one particular TOC. Therefore, it is essential that every member of the team works together in order to achieve the ultimate goal of providing a high quality rail service.

The recruitment staff will want to be certain that you can work effectively as part of a team, which is why you may be asked questions that relate to your team working experience.

There now follows a sample response to this question. Once you have read it, take time to construct your own response using the template provided.

SAMPLE RESPONSE – Can you tell me about a time when you have worked as part of a team to achieve a goal?

"Yes, I can. I like to keep fit and healthy and as part of this aim I play football for a local Sunday team. We had worked very hard to get to the cup final and we were faced with playing a very good opposition team who had recently won the league title. After only ten minutes of play, one of our players was sent off and we conceded a penalty as a result. Being one goal down and 80 minutes left to play we were faced with a mountain to climb. However, we all remembered our training and worked very hard in order to prevent any more goals being scored. Due to playing with ten players, I had to switch positions and play as a defender, something that I am not used to. The team worked brilliantly to hold off any further opposing goals and after 60 minutes we managed to get an equaliser. The game

went to penalties in the end and we managed to win the cup. I believe I am an excellent team player and can always be relied upon to work as an effective team member at all times. I understand that being an effective team member is very important if the Train Operating Company is to provide a high level of service to the passenger. However, above all of this, effective teamwork is essential in order to maintain the high safety standards that are set."

TEMPLATE FOR QUESTION 6 – CAN YOU TELL ME ABOUT A TIME WHEN YOU HAVE WORKED AS PART OF A TEAM TO ACHIEVE A GOAL?

QUESTION 7 – CAN YOU PROVIDE US WITH AN EXAMPLE OF A PROJECT YOU HAVE HAD TO COMPLETE AND THE OBSTACLES YOU HAD TO OVERCOME?

Having the ability to complete tasks and projects successfully demonstrates that you have the ability to complete your initial Train Conductor training course. Many people give up on things in life and fail to achieve their goals. The recruitment staff will need to be convinced that you are going to complete all training successfully and, if you can provide evidence of where you have already done this, then this will go in your favour.

When responding to this type of question, try to think of a difficult, drawn out task that you achieved despite a number of obstacles that were in your way. You may choose to use examples from your work life or even from some recent academic work that you have carried out. Take a look at the following sample question before using the template provided to construct your own response based on your own experiences.

SAMPLE RESPONSE – Can you provide us with an example of a project you have had to complete and the obstacles you had to overcome?

"Yes I can. I recently successfully completed a NEBOSH course (National Examination Board in Occupational Safety and Health) via distance learning. The course took two years to complete in total and I had to carry out all studying in my own time whilst holding down my current job.

The biggest obstacle I had to overcome was finding the time to complete the work to the high standard that I wanted to achieve. I decided to manage my time effectively and I allocated two hours every evening of the working week in

which to complete the work required. I found the time management difficult but I stuck with it and I was determined to complete the course. In the end I achieved very good results and I very much enjoyed the experience and challenge. I have a determined nature and I have the ability to concentrate for long periods of time when required. I can be relied upon to finish projects to a high standard."

TEMPLATE FOR QUESTION 7 – CAN YOU PROVIDE US WITH AN EXAMPLE OF A PROJECT YOU HAD TO COMPLETE AND THE OBSTACLE YOU HAD TO OVERCOME?

QUESTION 8 – CAN YOU PROVIDE US WITH AN EXAMPLE OF A SAFETY-RELATED TASK THAT YOU HAVE HAD TO PERFORM?

Safety is an extremely important part of the Train Conductors role and the recruitment staff need to know that you are capable of working safely at all times. The term 'safety' should be an integral part of some of your responses during the interview. Making reference to the fact that you are aware of the importance of safety at every opportunity is a positive thing. When responding to safety-related questions try to include examples where you have had to work to, or follow, safety guidelines or procedures. If you have a safety qualification then it is definitely worthwhile mentioning this during your interview. Any relevant safety experience or related role should also be discussed.

Now take a look at the following sample response before using the template provided to construct your own response.

SAMPLE RESPONSE – Can you provide us with an example of a safety-related task that you have had to perform?

"I currently work as a gas fitter and I am often required to perform safety-related tasks. An example of one of these tasks would involve the installation of gas-fired boilers. When fitting a gas boiler I have to ensure that I carry out a number of safety checks during the installation stage which ensures my work is safe and to a high standard. I have been trained, and I am qualified, to carry out my work in accordance with strict safety guidelines. I also have a number of safety certificates to demonstrate my competence.

I am fully aware that if I do not carry out my job in accordance with safety guidelines there is the possibility that somebody may become injured or even killed."

TEMPLATE FOR QUESTION 8 – CAN YOU PROVIDE US WITH AN EXAMPLE OF A SAFETY RELATED TASK THAT YOU HAVE HAD TO PERFORM?

Hopefully you are now starting to get a feel for how you need to respond to the interview questions. The following set of interview questions are further examples of questions you could get asked during the interviews.

QUESTION 9 – HOW DO YOU THINK YOU WOULD COPE WITH WORKING ON YOUR OWN AND UNSUPERVISED FOR LONG PERIODS?

Lone working is an unfortunate part of the Train Conductors job. You will spend many hours on your own and this can be a problem for many people. Even though you will be speaking to passengers on the train you will still be required to work unsupervised. You need to think carefully about this downside to the job. Can you cope with it? Do you have any experience of working on your own? If you do not then you will have to convince the panel that you can cope with it.

QUESTION 10 – WHAT IS YOUR SICKNESS RECORD LIKE AND WHAT DO YOU THINK IS AN ACCEPTABLE LEVEL OF SICKNESS?

Most employers detest sickness and they especially detest sickness that is not genuine. For every day that an employee is off sick will cost the TOC dearly. Therefore, they want to employ people who have a good sickness record. Obviously you cannot lie when responding to this question as the TOC will carry out checks. The latter part of the question is simple to answer. Basically no amount of sickness is acceptable but sometimes genuine sickness cannot be helped. Remember to tell them that you do not take time off sick unless absolutely necessary and you can be relied upon to come to work.

QUESTION 11 – HAVE YOU EVER WORKED DURING THE NIGHT AND HOW DO YOU FEEL ABOUT WORKING SHIFTS?

Train Conductors work irregular shifts and the Train Operating Company want to know that you can handle them. Speak to any person who works shifts and they will tell you that after a number of years they can start to take their toll. Remember to tell the panel that you are looking forward to working shifts and in particular night duties. If you can provide examples of where you have worked irregular shift patterns then remember to tell them.

QUESTION 12 – WOULD YOU GET BORED OF TRAVELLING THE SAME ROUTE DAY IN, DAY OUT?

Of course the only answer here is no! Yes, we would all probably get bored of the same journey every day, but don't tell them this.

QUESTION 13 – HOW MANY PEOPLE WORK FOR THIS TOC?

Questions that relate to facts and figures about the TOC might come up. They want to know that you are serious about joining them and that you are not just there to become a Train Conductor. Make sure you study their website and find out as much about them as possible.

QUESTION 14 – HOW MANY STATIONS DOES THE TRAIN OPERATING COMPANY SERVICE?

Once again, this is a question that relates to your knowledge of the TOC. This kind of information can usually be found by visiting their website. Please see our Useful Contacts section for more details.

QUESTION 15 – WHAT ARE THE MISSION AND AIMS OF THIS COMPANY?

Many organisations, including Train Operating Companies, set themselves aims and objectives. They usually relate to the high level of customer service that they promise to deliver. When you apply to become a Train Conductor you should not only prepare for each stage of the selection process but you should also learn as much as possible about the company you are applying to join. Learning this kind of information is important and it will demonstrate your seriousness about joining their particular company. Always remember this rule, working for the TOC comes first, becoming a Train Conductor comes second! Visit the website of the TOC in order to view their mission, aims, objectives or customer charter.

QUESTION 16 – CAN YOU PROVIDE US WITH AN EXAMPLE OF WHEN YOU HAVE HAD TO WORK IN AN EMERGENCY?

This question is also likely to be asked during the application form stage of the process. Being able to remain calm under pressure is very important and will form an integral part of your training. Maybe you have had to deal with an emergency at work or even in the home? Whatever example you decide to use, make sure you tell them that you stayed calm and focused on the task in hand. Make reference to the importance of safety during your response too.

QUESTION 17 – DO YOU THINK IT'S IMPORTANT FOR STAFF TO WEAR A UNIFORM?

The answer to this question should be yes. The reason for this is that a uniform gives customers and passenger's confidence in the service they are receiving. It is also important during an emergency situation so that customers know to turn to you,

the Train Conductor, for help and guidance. Uniforms are positive for the image of Train Operating Companies which is why they use them. Be positive about uniforms and tell them that you are looking forward to wearing one and taking pride in your appearance.

FINAL TIPS FOR PREPARING FOR THE INTERVIEWS

- Make sure you turn up to your interview on time! Find out the route to the interview location well in advance and make sure you don't get stuck in traffic or have any problems parking. Prepare for these eventualities well in advance.

- Wear formal clothing for your interview. Make sure you are clean-shaven and your shoes are clean and polished. Remember that you will be representing the company if you are successful and your appearance is very important.

- Visit the website of the TOC you are applying for and learn information about how they operate and what they are about. This is important so that you can create an image that you are serious about working for them and not just interested in becoming a Train Conductor.

- During your preparation for the interview, try to think of some recent examples of situations you have been in that are relevant to the role of a Train Conductor.

- When responding to the questions try to concentrate on what you have achieved so far during your life. It is important that you can demonstrate a track record of achievement.

- Make sure you smile during your interview. Sit up straight in the chair and do not fidget.

CHAPTER SEVEN

USEFUL CONTACTS

Within this section of the guide I have provided you with a list of Train Operating Companies that exist in England, Scotland and Wales. Please note, the list is not exhaustive and you may find other TOCs operating within your area/region. Some of the contact details may also change from time to time.

Arriva Trains Wales
St Mary's House
47 Penarth Road
Cardiff CF10 5DJ
0845 6061 660
www.arrivatrainswales.co.uk
customer.relations@arrivatrainswales.co.uk

C2C
10th Floor, 207 Old Street,
London EC1V 9NR

0845 6014873
www.c2c-online.co.uk
c2c.customerrelations@nationalexpress.com

Chiltern Railways
2nd floor, Western House
Rickfords Hill
Aylesbury, Buckinghamshire HP20 2RX
08456 005 165
www.chilternrailways.co.uk

CrossCountry
Cannon House
18 The Priory
Queensway, Birmingham B4 6BS
0870 010 0084
www.crosscountrytrains.co.uk
info@crosscountrytrains.co.uk

East Coast
East Coast House
25 Skeldergate House
York Y01 6DH
08457 225 225
www.eastcoast.co.uk

East Midlands Trains
1 Prospect Place
Millennium Way
Pride Park
Derby DE24 8HG
08457 125 678
www.eastmidlandstrains.co.uk
getintouch@eastmidlandstrains.co.uk

Eurostar

Times House
Bravingtons Walk
Regent Quarter
London N1 9AW
08701 606 600
www.eurostar.com

First Capital Connect

www.firstcapitalconnect.co.uk

First Great Western

Head Office
Milford House
1 Milford Street
Swindon SN1 1HL
08457 000 125
www.firstgreatwestern.co.uk

First Hull Trains

4th Floor
Europa House
184 Ferensway
Hull HU1 3UT
08456 769 905
www.hulltrains.co.uk

First TransPennine Express

Floor 7
Bridgewater House
60 Whitworth Street
Manchester M1 6LT
0845 600 1671
www.tpexpress.co.uk

Gatwick Express
Go Ahead House
26-28 Addiscombe Road
Croydon CR9 5GA
0845 850 15 30
www.gatwickexpress.com

Grand Central
River House
17 Museum Street
York YO1 7DJ
0845 6034852
www.grandcentralrail.co.uk
info@grandcentralrail.com

Heathrow Connect
www.heathrowconnect.com

Heathrow Express
6th Floor
50 Eastbourne Terrace
Paddington
London W2 6LX
020 8750 6600
www.heathrowexpress.com

Island Line Trains
Ryde St Johns Road Station,
Ryde, Isle of Wight
PO33 2BA
01983 812 591
www.southwesttrains.co.uk

London Midland

102 New Street
Birmingham B2 4JB
0121 634 2040
www.londonmidland.com
comments@londonmidland.com

London Overground

London Overground Rail Operations
125 Finchley Road
London NW3 6HY
0845 601 4867
www.tfl.gov.uk/overground

London Underground

www.tfl.gov.uk

Merseyrail

Rail House
Lord Nelson Street
Liverpool L1 1JF
0151 702 2534
www.merseyrail.org

National Express East Anglia

Floor One
Oliver's Yard
55 City Road
London EC1Y 1HQ
0845 600 7245
www.nationalexpresseastanglia.com
nxea.customerrelations@nationalexpress.com

Northern Rail
Northern House
9 Rougier Street
York YO1 6HZ
0845 00 00 125
www.northernrail.org
customer.relations@northernrail.org

ScotRail
Atrium Court
50 Waterloo Street
Glasgow G2 6HQ
08700 005151
www.scotrail.co.uk

South West Trains
Friars Bridge Court
41-45 Blackfriars Road
London SE1 8NZ
08700 00 5151
www.southwesttrains.co.uk

Southeastern
Customer Services
PO Box 63428
London SE1P 5FD
0845 000 2222
www.southeasternrailway.co.uk

Stansted Express
www.stanstedexpress.com

Virgin Trains
85 Smallbrook
Queensway
Birmingham B5 4HA
0845 000 8000
www.virgintrains.co.uk

Wrexham & Shropshire
The Pump House
Coton Hill
Shrewsbury SY1 2DP
0845 260 5233
www.wrexhamandshropshire.co.uk
info@wrexhamandshropshire.co.uk

OTHER USEFUL WEBSITES

Rail Safety & Standards Board
www.rssb.co.uk

The Department for Transport
www.dft.gov.uk

Rail Technical Pages
www.railway-technical.com

how2become

Visit www.how2become.com
to find more titles and courses
that will help you to pass
the Train Conductor selection
process, including:

- How to pass job interview books and DVD's.

- Train Driver books, DVD's and courses.

- Psychometric testing books and CD's.

www.how2become.com

Printed in Great Britain
by Amazon